RUN, RUN AS FAST AS YOU CAN.

Peter Cleary

Note for Librarians: A cataloguing record for this book is available from Library and Archives Canada at www.collectionscanada.ca/amicus/index-e.html

Printed in Victoria, BC, Canada.

ISBN: 978-1-4269-0-9597 (sc)

ISBN: 978-1-4269-0-9610 (e-book)

We at Trafford believe that it is the responsibility of us all, as both individuals and corporations, to make choices that are environmentally and socially sound. You, in turn, are supporting this responsible conduct each time you purchase a Trafford book, or make use of our publishing services. To find out how you are helping, please visit www.trafford.com/responsiblepublishing.html

Our mission is to efficiently provide the world's finest, most comprehensive book publishing service, enabling every author to experience success. To find out how to publish your book, your way, and have it available worldwide, visit us online at www.trafford.com

Trafford rev. 6/26/2009

Cover design by the author's son Andrew Cleary, cover photograph taken by the author on the road to Khorixas, Namibia.

 www.trafford.com

North America & international
toll-free: 1 888 232 4444 (USA & Canada)
phone: 250 383 6864 ♦ fax: 250 383 6804 ♦ email: info@trafford.com

The United Kingdom & Europe
phone: +44 (0)1865 487 395 ♦ local rate: 0845 230 9601
facsimile: +44 (0)1865 481 507 ♦ email: info.uk@trafford.com

10 9 8 7 6 5 4 3 2 1

Contents

Preface.

In January 2008 I woke early one morning and started to write a book. In the next six weeks I wrote ten thousand words a week and almost finished it.

How do you explain such an outpouring in your sixty fourth year?

Part of the explanation lies in the sale of our main business in April of 2007. For the first time in a working life spanning almost forty years I had some time.

Then a friend gave me a CD of a talk given by a modern English poet and I was captivated by his philosophy and the beauty of the language. For the first time since the 1960's I spent time reading poetry.

In September 2007 I wrote this first simple poem;

I remember.

*In my later days the exquisite writings of others
have brought about a rebirth of emotion more
refined than the versions of my youth.*

And I remember.

I remember the huge snake rearing high
above the tall grass
and the fear that would not allow me to return
to that place.

I remember the confined space of the old miner's tunnel
holding me captive
and the fright when the torchlight
revealed panicked bats and a civet defiant in its fear.

I remember the mountains of cloud building towards evening
and the many days of dry lightning
before that wondrous moment
when the fat rain brought the clean smell of wetness.

I hope this remembering in my later days
will fulfil early desires.

Those memories were of a boy on a farm ten kilometres west of Bulawayo, Rhodesia.

In the next few months a dozen poems followed, most of them stimulated by intense personal events in my life.

And that is what the book is about; the intense personal experiences of my life and work in the motor industry.

The book is in three main sections, the first dealing with Ford Motor Company from 1970, the second the time I spent with Mercedes-Benz from 1981 and the last my days in the motor dealerships I started in 1995.

I had a wonderful time writing it and the act of writing certainly fulfilled early desires.

PART ONE

Ford Motor Company.

Chapter 1.

Getting started.

I was jealous of my housemate, Bruce Gillmer.

We were renting a cottage at Amsterdam Hoek on the Swartkops River, a tidal estuary some 20 kilometres north of Port Elizabeth. In the morning I'd walk two hundred metres to where my 1956 model Peugeot was parked on a hill because the battery was defective, start it by rolling down the hill, and drive 25 kilometres to Victoria Park High School. I had started teaching English to pay off the bursary I'd received from the Cape Education Department.

Bruce would go to the Neave Assembly Plant of Ford Motor Company where he had started as a graduate trainee in the training section of the Salaried Personnel Department.

In the evening we would compare notes over a few beers. It was no contest

The year was 1970.

I really had no idea what I wanted to do with my life in those days. I had completed a BA honours degree in English at Rhodes University but if I was honest I was more interested in rugby and in student activism at the end when I was on the Students' Representative Council.

If I had a wish, it was to write and I half-heartedly pursued this by breaking away from my studies in 1967 to work as a newspaper reporter with the "Herald" in Port Elizabeth. I had argued with myself that I would never be a writer unless I practiced the trade; but the newspaper business was too cynical for me.

If I had a love, it was about motor cars. Thanks to Bruce I could envisage the acrid smells and metallic noises of a vast assembly plant making those wonderful Cortinas and Escorts and Fairlanes and F-Series trucks.

Eventually I asked him to arrange an interview for me. It wasn't going to be that easy to quit the school. I'd have to pay back the bursary, and give them a fair notice period, but the lure of the motor industry was very strong.

I was interviewed by Dirk Pieterse who was then managing the recruitment section of salaried personnel. Some things stick in my mind; he asked what I knew about the motor industry and I said nothing really unless he wanted me to quote Bruce verbatim. He asked what I wanted to do and I said I wanted to sell cars. "We don't do that", he said, "We have dealers who do that." "Oh", I said," I'd like to work in the marketing department helping the dealers to sell the cars."

I also had my own concerns. I wanted to know how the motor industry was going to evolve as there was only enough oil to last another 20 years (I'm still asking myself the same question, 38 years later!)

It was pretty naïve stuff from me but we got on well. We

were of a similar age and had similar values. Eventually he marched me into his boss' office.

Don Scott was not much older than me but already the manager of the Salaried Personnel department. As well as recruitment he was responsible for organization planning, job evaluation, salaried administration and training. He was an outstanding manager, and my first hero and mentor. Unfortunately he was to leave quite soon after I joined.

About three hours later they made their pronouncement; I was perfect for salaried personnel! I was to be offered a position as a graduate trainee even though the graduate programme ran for a calendar year and I was only able to start in July, mid-way through the programme.

They did me the honour of offering me the job on the spot. I accepted in the same fashion

CHAPTER 2.

First test.

For the first weeks at Ford Motor Company I walked tall.

This was despite the fact that the offices of the Salaried Personnel Department, my department, were not in a very prestigious spot next to the canteen and that I was doing the most menial job in the department.

It was a test.

I was to learn that all grad trainees were started in the job of salary clerk to find out whether they could handle repetitive tasks with discipline and accuracy.

There were around 1300 salaried people at Ford Motor Company in South Africa at that time. The salary clerk had to record, manually, all changes in status of those people. They could join, be promoted, demoted, have a salary increase or decrease, go on pension or die. In each case the department concerned would inform me and I would inform payroll and change all the records.

Not a great job, but I was on fire.

My joy was increased when I found that most of my

contemporaries had been at Rhodes University with me. In the 70's Ford was hiring around 10 new graduate trainees a year and most of the recruitment was done from the local universities, Rhodes in Grahamstown and later the University of Port Elizabeth.

This had the added advantage of bringing in people with similar cultural values so that communication and teamwork were immediately enhanced. This only happened in the Sales and Marketing, Finance and Industrial Relations departments, as the two local universities did not have engineering faculties, the kind of people we needed in production and engineering.

I was to find a very different culture when I moved into Product Development years later, and only then truly understood the advantages of having staff with common values.

I passed the test in two months and was ready for my next assignment.

The other lesson I learnt was that it is not so smart to blood your grad trainees on an essential administrative job. The person who replaced me had made a muck of it and four months later I was asked to sort it out. I wrote a process for the actions required, and the document was used for years until computerisation was introduced.

It was a measure of my intensity in those first days at Ford that I was able to recall the 40-something processes for the salary clerk job without consulting any documents.

CHAPTER 3.

Learning about organizations.

American companies are great at logistics and controlling, and they are great at organization planning.

The biggest value I got from my short time in Salaried Personnel was an understanding of how to organise work and rank jobs. It has held me in good stead all of my working life and I'm grateful that this was my first real job in the industry.

My assignment was in the position of Organisation Planning Analyst, responsible to evaluate job ranking and organization change proposals received from other departments in the company.

But first I had to undergo another test.

The basic organisation and ranking of jobs in South Africa was established by Ed Valentine, an American who came out on this assignment in 1965. The "Valentine Study" was our bible (and much hated by the many aggrieved parties who believed their jobs were worth more). Valentine identified some 400 different positions.

The trouble was all these high-flying grad trainees again. The records were a shambles.

Don Scott gave me the assignment to update the master schedule on job titles and ranking levels. He made a production of it, giving me the assignment in the bullpen, in front of my workmates. He told me no one had completed this assignment correctly and I would likely also fail. He gave me a month to complete the work.

I was very focused the next few days and right through the weekend and I went to him on the Monday of the following week, four working days after being given the assignment, and said I was finished.

That provoked great hilarity, and all of the staff and managers who had worked in the Organisation and Management Planning Section were called in to find how many mistakes I'd made. As well as Don, Dirk Pieterse was there, as was Brian Robinson, then head of the organization section, and my mates from Rhodes, Jay Owens, Doc Seiler, Sean Bownes and Tim Ford.

They could not find a single error.

I don't think anything I did at Ford made a bigger impact on my reputation and career than that single four day and a weekend job.

It also brought me to my first meeting with Fred Ferreirra, Director of Industrial Relations who had obviously been told of the success. Don reminded me on the way to the hallowed directors' offices on the 17th floor of Ford House that this was an American company and I was to greet everyone, even the Managing Director, by their Christian names; I failed that test.

Fred Ferreirra was a distant and disconcerting figure, perhaps befitting the man who also had responsibility for handling labour and union matters. He was rumoured to have impressed his American bosses by his relationship with senior government people and in that way had received his director's position. If you believed the rumours you would miss the shrewdness and competence.

The whole time I was talking Fred stared at me, obviously not interested in the content of what I was saying. Eventually he stopped me with a question "What is that accent, are you English?" I explained that I grew up in Rhodesia but he probably knew that; he had succeeded in throwing me off balance.

I was never comfortable in Fred Ferreirra's office.

One of the greatest difficulties in ranking a job is understanding the difference between staff and line. How do you give a production foreman, supervising a section of the assembly line, with maybe 25 people working for him, the same ranking as a financial planning analyst responsible for just himself and the production of his brain? I could justify it, and believed it, but often could not sell it.

I remember a proposal I worked on for the Truck Assembly Plant. The proposal had been submitted by the plant manager Gert Burger. Gert was held in high regard not only as a production manager but also as a clever man. He held a degree in mechanical engineering. He was also a toughie.

He had a great deal of difficulty understanding why this youngster with an arts degree could be given the responsibility to approve his organisation.

He insisted that I come to his plant in Deal Party three Friday afternoons in a row to sit with him and hear his ideas about his people and his plant (and general philosophy about everything it turned out) before we considered his proposal.

I learnt a lot from him and it turned out OK.

My next assignment was in recruitment, interviewing people applying for jobs at Ford. I was lousy at it. Today I make sure I have the opinion of a number of people before I employ someone, and if applicable the candidate should also be interviewed by the people they will be working with.

Chapter 4.

First lessons in managing.

I was the first graduate trainee at Ford South Africa to be given the responsibility for a management position during their trainee year, even though in my case the appointment was temporary. The position was supervisor of Organisation and Management Planning.

I was thrilled, but I was also aggrieved. I wish I could say I was aggrieved for noble reasons but it was a little more basic than that. When you reached management you could lease a car, and I badly wanted to drive a Capri. I had already bought my first and only new car (for the rest of my working life somebody else owned the car), a base model Escort, the one with the cardboard door trims.

Ford was a great training company in the 70's. Many of the top managers in the other motor companies started their careers at Ford. I spend more time on this subject in a later chapter but my own experience shows the possibilities for development; I was with Ford for 11 years, and held 14 jobs in Port Elizabeth, Johannesburg, Detroit, London and Melbourne.

I would never have received such great experience if I'd been promoted from the grad trainee programme directly into a management position as that would have limited my ability to move sideways. I know that now and I'm grateful that my managers resisted the pressure I put on them

I was about to receive an extremely valuable lesson in the management of people. My section was a small one and I had two people working for me, Jay Owens and Johnny Koeman. Both were social science graduates, Jay had an honours degree, Johnny a masters.

Neither of them had analytical and writing skills at a level needed for an Organisation Planning analyst. The work came naturally to me and I was frustrated by their lack of progress. Commitments I was making to the departments who had submitted proposals, and to my management, were not being met.

Eventually, without letting Johnny and Jay know my intentions I spoke to my boss about it and requested that their time in my section be shortened and they be replaced with more suitable candidates. The boss was the head of Salaried Personnel, Brian Robinson, who had replaced Don Scott.

This was not a decent thing to do. The programmes for the trainees were carefully mapped out, and although it was always understood that some would excel in certain jobs and not others, it was important to the understanding of any job in Industrial Relations that you receive training in key sections. Organisation planning was critical to the understanding of the scope of the company and the jobs within it.

The first mistake was not consulting with them and trying

to work out a plan of action which gave them a clean record. I consoled myself with the fact that I had spoken to them of my dissatisfaction on many of the jobs they did; but I was kidding myself if I thought I'd tried hard enough.

But an even bigger lesson was to come.

Johnny Koeman became the best Training Manager Ford had during my time with them. He had compassion for people and a real interest in developing them to their full potential. Jay Owens became a university lecturer and the last time I worked with him he was teaching at the Wits Business School.

Ever since I've tried to understand where a person could be better employed if they did not have the aptitude for a particular job.

CHAPTER 5

Marketing Strategy.

I finally got into the marketing Department. My new boss was someone I had known under rather different circumstances.

I was still in the under 20 division when I played my first game of rugby for the Rhodes University first team. It was not going to be an easy debut, our opponents were the champion team of the previous year, Parks, and the venue was the Boet Erasmus Stadium, the largest rugby grounds in Port Elizabeth, and in those days still a test venue.

I played on the wing and Kingsley Amm was my centre. We were just into the game when I received the ball and a heavy tackle simultaneously. I must have lain on the ground for a second or two longer than necessary because I was unceremoniously lifted to my feet by the jersey and Kingsley said to me "Stay on your feet, you're in the first team now".

And this was my new boss.

Kingsley Amm and Don Scott were the two best examples of the perfect manager in my early career. Kingsley had a lot of self-assurance; it was something I first noticed on the rugby field, he seemed to know what to do and others looked to him for leadership. He had no need for self-promotion, a wonderful attribute in a big corporation because he let his people take credit if they deserved it. And he had big match temperament, he wasn't afraid of anyone if he was in the right.

I was a Marketing Strategy Analyst. It was my job to look after a number of car models, in my case Cortina and Fairlane. I had to know their market segment and competitors, know the features and pricing of all the models in that segment, predict likely new model developments and market trends, make recommendations for price and model changes, brief the advertising agencies and assist in the development of promotional material and launches.

There were two others doing the same job on other models and on accessories, and another section in our department was responsible for sales planning; forecasting production and sales for the months ahead.

I was delighted to be working with Des Bramwell, one of my closest friends from Rhodes. Des and I sat at the same table in the canteen the first day we arrived at university. We sat with eight others and the ten of us stayed together for three years.

Des developed into one of the best promotional people I knew. He had the knack of pushing the right buttons of the dealers to get the best sales improvement. He and another colleague Malcolm McClelland (who was later to be one of my Region Managers when I ran Field Operations) had developed a salesman's guide to the features and benefits of our models and competitors which they called "MI5, Know Your Enemy".

We were passionately involved in our work. It was here that I developed the habit of staying after hours to debate issues relating to my job. One of those issues was whether to drop the Capri (I never got to lease one!).

The Ford Capri was a spectacularly styled and priced car. Like the Mustang in the U.S. it came from nowhere; it didn't replace a previous model. Of course it was a powder puff sports car relying more on style than performance, although one of our dealers, Basil Green, did conversions in which he installed V8 engines and totally changed the character of the car.

Capri sold in economically viable volumes for many years, but the bloom was off, it was not to be replaced in Europe, and we had to consider keeping it for its image value. After weeks of argument we recommended it be discontinued.

One of my Cortina models was the station wagon. When I got into the analysis I could not help noticing what a wonderful opportunity existed for this model. There were very few competitors, the segment was large at 6% of the total market (not much smaller than the SUV market in South Africa today) and it was dominated by an ageing car, the Peugeot 404. From the popularity of the Peugeot it was clear that the main purpose of station wagons in the country was for representatives to carry samples of their goods.

I made recommendations on features with appeal to this buyer group, wrote bulletins of information and motivation to dealers and came into conflict with an important person; Robin Field.

Robin Field was the Advertising Manager. He had done the job for many years with distinction and was a true professional. He had also developed a tough crust to stop all the advertising experts in the company, from the Managing Director downwards, changing the ads.

When I got to manage advertising I understood what a fine job he did running interference for the agency. But at that time I had issue with him; he would not run ads for my station wagon.

My argument was simple; there was clearly no awareness of the Cortina station wagon so how was I to grow our share without advertising. I had this analogy that if you grew up in a sphere you could never conceive of anything square; he wasn't impressed.

In retrospect, he was quite decent to me although I did not get my ads.

CHAPTER 6.

Fairlane launch.

New product launches were very simple affairs in the early 70's, specially for low volume models such as the Australian designed Ford Fairlane.

There were no promotional companies specialising in dealer and media launches and such events were generally handled by the motor companies or their advertising agencies.

Despite the relatively low-key approach, my first launch was going to be special.

Robin Field asked me to brief the agency on the market and product background on the new Fairlane model we were to launch in a few months. It would be my first introduction to an advertising agency, quite an occasion for a young marketing man.

The Australian sourced large cars were in a difficult market area already dominated by Mercedes-Benz and BMW. They offered more space and power at lower prices but the quality and mechanical reliability were not of the same standard.

And with all of that power and a live rear axle, gravel roads became an adventure.

A few weeks later we were invited to the agency's offices across the road from Ford House to see their proposals for advertising and promotional material. Kingsley could not make it and asked that I get their ideas for a dealer launch, something we had discussed without any firm ideas coming to the fore.

I can only remember the emotion not the content of that first agency presentation. It was not a big deal for them as the spend on Fairlane was tiny compared to our volume models Cortina and Escort. Nevertheless there is always that element of showmanship and glamour in an agency presentation, much heightened for me as it was a first.

I was impressed and went straight into Kingsley's office and reported what I had seen and also told him I had cracked the idea for the launch. The conversation went something like this;

"Is this the agency's idea?"

"No, it's mine; I haven't talked to them about it yet, or to Robin. I wanted to get your take on it first".

"So tell me".

"We re-enact what I've just experienced with the agency, like a play. We present the features and market information and volumes to the agency on the stage, but we're actually doing it for the dealers. Then we reveal the car and have a break for viewing, and then the agency replies and shows us, but really the dealers, the advertising, brochures, promotional material for their showrooms and ideas for their own launches. I think it would be really good, and the dealers would love the glitz of the agency presentation. What do you think?"

"I really like it. I think it can work. Who would do the Ford presentation?"

"I would".

"Come on Pete, you've only been here a few months, no-one is going to buy putting you up in front of the dealers?"

Eventually he agreed that I could present my ideas to John Dill, the director, and other senior sales and marketing managers. If they liked my idea, and if I sold myself well enough, he'd ask them, after I'd left the room, whether they agreed to me doing the Ford side of the presentation.

That was Kingsley. He did not need to use the launch to promote himself, he would be quite happy if one of his people used the event for their own growth and development. I'm sure he sold them on the idea after I left the room.

I had earned my first crack at stardom!

It was agreed to launch Fairlane on a regional basis. We were to do presentations in Port Elizabeth, Cape Town, Durban, Bloemfontein and Johannesburg. It would also serve as an introduction to the dealers of Doug Kitterman who had recently arrived from the States to take over the MD's job, and Ian Hepworth, the National Sales Manager would do the introductions.

A few experiences remain with me.

In Durban we did the presentation at the Lansdown, a hotel just back of the beaches. The conference room was on the same floor as one of the parking floors so we could drive the show car directly into the room; we papered the opening so that the car could dramatically break through when I finished my bit and said "Let's look at the car now".

The car wouldn't start. In the room we could hear the starter motor grinding without success and then the paper heaved inwards and slowly tore as they pushed the car into the room.

Ian Hepworth chose that evening to take the young man under his wing, as he would have put it. Ian was strictly old-school and he ran the sales regions like they were his private fiefdom, brooking no change to his tried and tested ways. I had been warned that if he liked me he would invite me to have a few drinks with him, which would turn out to be a whisky fest. Luckily the next day was a rest day.

Our last launch was in Johannesburg, the most important of all of the venues as half the market and dealers were in the Transvaal. We flew in that morning from Bloemfontein and could not land! The airport was covered in fog. We returned to Bloemfontein and Ian started drinking bloody marys at 10 in the morning. I nervously walked round and round the departure lounge.

Eventually we got into Johannesburg timeously and the presentation went off well; I'm sure I was the only one who heard the slurring in Ian's voice.

The assembly quality of the first Fairlanes produced was shocking and an embarrassment to Kitterman. He did not join us in Bloemfontein as he'd returned to Port Elizabeth to hold crisis meetings with plant management.

In Johannesburg he announced that we were withdrawing all the Fairlanes produced thus far, and would only supply when he was happy with the quality. The cars already produced would be absorbed into the company fleet. It was a decision which found much favour among dealers who had been complaining about quality levels in general for some time; here was a man who could do something about it.

And that's how I got to drive a Ford Fairlane 500 for R15 a month.

Chapter 7.

Getting on the wrong side of powerful people.

Most of the requests for new models, or changes to present models are initiated by Marketing either from their own market studies and research, or from customer's wants transmitted through the dealer network.

One of these requests was to introduce a two-door model in the Escort range.

Although a two-door car was available in Britain the process to introduce the car in South Africa takes some time, particularly with a local content programme where the impact on changed parts needs detailed study, and might need procuring tooling. At the very end the order pipeline itself was 6 months.

None of us had been around when Marketing initiated the request for the two-door Escort. But the decision was about to have a nasty chapter and I was going to be in the middle of it.

Neither Kingsley nor our sales planning guy were going to

be available for the monthly sales planning review, a meeting chaired by the MD and attended by the directors and top management in Product Development, Manufacturing and Finance. Sales and Marketing did the presentation. The upcoming meeting was to include our initial orders for the two-door Escort.

I was asked to do the presentation. We had a pre-meeting in John Dill's office. We did not believe the new Escort model had the potential indicated in the initial study and were projecting significantly lower volumes, which was sure to draw strong opposition. Kingsley was concerned that my first appearance at this directors standing meeting would be damaging to me. Dill said he would be at the meeting and would ensure that did not happen.

The reaction was much stronger than anticipated, and it came from Spence Sterling who was then Chief Engineer.

Let me give some background to this man who was to feature prominently in my life at Ford. Spence was a self-made man. He came from the southern suburbs of Johannesburg and received a bursary to complete a degree in mechanical engineering. He had a meteoric rise and when he was appointed Engine Plant Manager in South Africa he was the youngest in the Ford world to do so (I think he was 28).

Spence was a driven man, of exceptional ability, and you did not want to get in his way in his drive to the top. He was also a physically powerful man and comparisons with Sylvester Stallone would not be out of order.

The opening salvo was from Sterling, but it was reasonably mild. Then Brian Pitt, the Finance Director, entered the fray; Finance hate low cost models; any substitution from the more expensive models deteriorates profit. He said at this volume maybe the model should be canned.

That was when Spence got nasty, probably irked by Pitt holding a different opinion, but mostly due to his disrespect for John Dill. He reminded everyone how much work had gone into having this model approved and then launched into a diatribe into how useless and pathetic the Marketing department was. Somewhere in there I think my name was mentioned, certainly my inexperience, but I was literally in a state of shock at the vehemence of his attack.

Then came the piece de resistance; because he could not rely on Marketing his product planning people had done a study and one-third of C-class (Ford-speak for the small car market) segment sales were two-door models. He expected us to forecast at least this mix.

Kitterman looked at me and asked for my point of view. I tried to catch John Dill's eye but he wasn't going to help me.

I tried to couch my reply diplomatically. I said something like this; "Mr. Sterling is right, about one-third of C-class sales are two-door models. But this is because of the dominance of the Beetle which is only available as a two-door. If you look at the models which offer both two and four doors the percentage is closer to 10%"

Kitterman backed Sterling, we ordered the higher volume and the car was soon in trouble in the market. After a few years of spending money on distress merchandising the two-door Escort was eventually dropped.

A first doubt entered my soul.

CHAPTER 8.

Market research.

I became convinced that I would never be an outstanding marketing practioner if I did not understand market research.

Not that I would choose market research as a profession (like my son Andrew has done in the field of social research). I needed to know how market research could help me to understand customer needs, and advertising effectiveness, and media choices and many other subjects, and I was reading books on the subject.

My academic training was in English literature and I read avidly to teach myself the art of the exciting profession I had chosen. It is a habit I have never lost and has been most beneficial in my own businesses where I could try the new ideas I learnt. I never go into a bookstore (my favourite kind of store) without visiting the business books section.

I discussed my ideas with Kingsley who was less than enthusiastic. From his point of view I might get into a dead end because of the structure of market research in Ford of

South Africa. It was a one man band, it had dual reporting to local management and to Overseas Marketing Research in Detroit, and top management paid lip service to it.

He wasn't wrong. The present incumbent, Paul Stead, was one of our social circle, an outstanding marketing thinker but with a cynical and superior demeanour with which he battered those he did not rate. Much of his cynicism derived from senior management not using the information he was providing to them.

I didn't care about the destructive side of Paul's nature. He was giving me insights into marketing that no-one else could teach me. I remember one evening, in one of our interminable discussions about our business, Paul told us what he was learning by studying the cigarette advertising of Anton Rupert's organization.

He brought out a pack of Rothmans and a shaft of ads to prove his point. The use of royal language "prince of..." the use of rich colours, deep blues and purples, buying up back pages of magazines years in advance, using a special technique of etching to get superior print quality in newspaper advertising. Fascinating stuff.

Paul saw my interest as a means to move himself to another assignment. In one of those weird and sometimes brilliant development moves at Ford, a senior Supply man, Harry Doeg, was moved into the top job in marketing. Paul concentrated his considerable powers on persuading Harry to transfer me to be his understudy.

At the gathering after the Fairlane launch in Port Elizabeth he was in a huddle with Harry and they called me over. The conversation was about how qualified I was for market research. I couldn't see the connection, I had just showed a degree of competence in a presentation, market research was another animal altogether.

Eventually he got his way, and so did I.

Two weeks after I joined the market research department Paul Stead resigned to join the advertising agency, and a week later I was flying first class to Brazil.

Chapter 9.

Car clinic in Sao Paulo.

I arrived at one of Sao Paulo's two airports at night, with the exchange counters closed, and no-one to meet me. Not an auspicious start to my first trip outside southern Africa.

I'd read that the one airport was a long way out of town. So I needed to get a taxi driver to give me the price of the fare so that I could not get ripped off and waste Ford's money. And I needed to get one of them to understand that I only had traveler's cheques for US Dollars but I would exchange them and pay at the hotel. It doesn't sound as hard as it turned out.

We got to the hotel and I wasn't booked in, and they had no room!

It got sorted out. They paid off the taxi, found me a room for the night, exchanged some money and my contact, the Market Research manager for Brazil, got me on the phone, said he'd been at the other airport and arranged to collect me at 10 the next morning, Sunday, to spend the day at the coast.

It had been a roller coaster and tired as I was, I needed quite a few beers before I felt in control

I was out of control again the next day because of the language barrier. My host picked me up in a big American sedan and I sat in the front between him and his wife. In the back were two young children and a girl in her late teens. It turned out that the older girl was the nanny.

We drove down to Santos and through that city to the coast where we ended in a queue waiting for the ferry to a nearby island where they had a beach house. I had my first lesson in racial tolerance, Brazil style. The day was oppressively hot and humid and there was an old black man sitting on the sea wall. They invited him into the airconditioned car and they cheerfully squeezed up on the back seat.

My host was charming and cultured and very happy to share information with me. That was fortunate for me because I wanted to know everything. What about this old guy in the back?

It turned out that there were over a million people of African extraction in Brazil, a similar number of people of Asian descent and not too many of the original Indian people. The bulk of the people were of mixed blood. At the top of the pile were those who had retained their European line and culture. He was one of them, and I was able to witness their wealth and that of their friends at their home on the island that day.

Everyone was charming and wanted to engage me in conversation despite not having more than a dozen words of English. On the beach they erected a large awning and the three or four families all fitted under it. We were drinking a mixture of Tequila and a fruit juice in fairly large quantities.

When I sought relief in the sea I found it was warmer than blood.

It was an adventurous day but I was very glad to get into my room at the correct hotel, the Othon Palace. I had a big day the next day, I was to meet my American boss (turns out he was Canadian) for the first time.

Jim McKinnon was then in his mid forties; a short stocky man with sandy hair and a no-nonsense attitude. In the months I was to work directly with him it was all business. The only socializing we did was when he invited me to attend an ice hockey game with him in Detroit. I never knew if he had a family. I sometimes wondered if, being Canadian, he had to be more American than the Americans.

We met at the offices of the market research company hired to do the car clinic. The owner of the business used his doctorate in his title, a practice I was to also find when I worked with the Germans years later. He looked like a plumper and older version of Rossano Brazzi when he played the role of the planter in South Pacific. It was clear that he left his business to his staff and there were two other men in the meeting who were managing the clinic.

The one was an Englishman with a calm aura who had spent a decade in South America, starting with a research agency in Venezuela so that he spoke both Spanish and Portuguese. The other was an interesting young American who had come to Brazil on an American Field Service contract and had been posted to Manaus in the middle of the Amazon jungle. There he met an exquisite lady and married her, and she was struggling to acclimatise to the cold weather in Sao Paulo!

McKinnon was finding fault in the arrangements and was being abrupt to the point of rudeness. They handled him very well and accommodated his requirements. Then the two foreign nationals took us off to visit the site where the clinic was to be held, starting the next day.

A car clinic is used to test a number of things. They can be used early in the design process to test varying designs, or bodystyles. They are often used to test the reaction to alternative models, sometimes models that came from different parts of the world. They can also be used to test pricing assumptions and the desirability of different features.

Respondents who are in the target market; that is people who had bought a similar car new in the recent past, are invited to the venue at specific times and told they will be viewing new models. This is enough inducement to most people but sometimes gifts need to be given to get attendance.

The models you want to test are displayed along with competitor cars. In order not to get any bias, all cars need to be of the same exterior colour and the seating material should be similar. All insignia is removed. Sometimes the cars displayed are fibre glass models (as was the case in this clinic) which look exactly like the real thing but which need hostesses to open and close the doors because they have a different sound and feel.

Respondents look at and sit in all of the cars and rate what they see and feel on a questionnaire. They are then given another questionnaire which lists the basic specifications and they are asked for pricing estimates and purchase intention. There can be another section with manufacturer and model identified.

Our clinic was held at a critical time for the Brazilian market. It had been a fairly closed market because exceptionally high levels of local content were required. The VW Beetle dominated with over 40% market share. The market was to be opened up, and the country was also opening up; at that time there was not even a decent road system between Sao Paulo and Rio de Janeiro, the two biggest cities.

Ford was considering building the next Pinto model in Brazil, and this car, in two versions, were the fibre glass models in the clinic. A bigger car, the Maverick, was also to be tested although it was in a slightly higher class. The competitor cars included new models anticipated from Volkswagen and other brands, and already on the market in Europe.

Here are some of the things that excited or scared my brain enough to be remembered.

One night I was asked to close up. I had no clue where in the city I was but I would simply flag a taxi. Half an hour later, and some six or seven flagging's later I was getting a little rattled. The scene was the same for all of them; I would open the passenger door and say "Othon Palace, per favor", he would shake his head and say "no". I was starting to think about the need to return to the venue and lock myself in for the night when I got a lift. I figured out later that it must have been the last ride for the day and if I wasn't going their way I wasn't going to get a ride.

The hostesses were a most beautiful group of young women and obviously politically correct (also needed to not have bias) because they ranged from light to dark skinned and with features typical of almost the whole world. They had probably been recruited from a modeling school.

Jim was analyzing some results every night and relaying them to the product planners in Detroit. They ordered an additional line of enquiry and a questionnaire needed to be changed. The agency had worked on it overnight but the questionnaires were not yet delivered to the clinic. I was working at the agency and Jim phoned me and ordered me to tell the owner of the business that if they were not there by the opening hour he would not pay them for the day and would never use them again.

Pretty tough stuff and not my style. I went to the owner and said something like this, "I'm sure you know Mr. McKinnon pretty well and know he can be a little strong. I ask you to please move heaven and earth to get those questionnaires to the clinic in time because I think he will be difficult to live with if you don't". Different approach, fortunately for me the same result.

Setting up a clinic is enormously expensive and a decision was taken to fly in respondents from neighbouring Argentina rather than move the show. They were offered free air tickets and the further inducement of a free night and meal in Sao Paulo. The agency received numerous skeptical calls from wives and girlfriends confirming the purpose. They had reason to be skeptical; the Argentinean group was far more aggressive and macho and gave the hostesses a hard time. I doubted the validity of their ratings as their minds were on other matters.

We had one sample group test the cars with a German-sourced Taunus on display. The car was in the market in Europe at the time and was probably recognizable to most of the sample. The response was strong and clear, the Brazilian's preferred European to American designs by a mile. I never found out why that information was not actioned, it could easily have been economic factors.

We had a product planner from Detroit with us and he was not a good advertisement for the caliber of people in that department. One night over dinner he raised an argument that reminded me of the Spence Sterling two-door Escort incident.

"This is all nonsense, you know" he said. "We need to design a new car for this market with an air-cooled engine at the back".

I thought he was joking but the expression said otherwise.

"Do you really think they buy the Beetle because of those features. You don't think it's got something to do with price, or reliability, or the cost of spare parts, or habit. Look at the taxis, do you think they like removing the front passenger seat and have their passengers crawl through to the back?"

When you get older you learn not to waste time like that. And I'm sure that would have been McKinnon's advice; he had an amused look on his face.

CHAPTER 10.

Detroit.

The Friday we left Sao Paulo the temperature soared to over 40 degrees Celsius, and we heard later that people died of heat exhaustion. We landed at Kennedy airport in New York at 14 degrees below. We waited outside for the bus to our terminal for almost ten minutes, and I rued the decision I had made to only buy warm clothing when I got to Detroit.

In Detroit Jim did his anti-social thing and said goodbye, see you in the office on Monday. No offer of a lift, no offer to take me to collect my assigned car the next day.

A taxi took me to the Holiday Inn on Michigan Avenue, Dearborn, the place that was to be home to me for months to come. That afternoon I slogged across the double lane of ice and snow to a store and bought a winter outfit.

The next morning, with keen anticipation, I was off to Ford's headquarters about five kilometers down Michigan Avenue to get a car. The building had the grandiose name of World Head Quarters and around 2000 employees worked in it.

In a way I was glad to be in the building on the Sunday with few people around so that I could get my bearings. In the lobby there were information boards and I read with interest the variety of functions performed, up to Mr. Ford's office on the top floor. I found where I needed to report the next day, and where the underground courtesy car park was located.

I filled in all of the forms and was led to this very large yellow Ford LTD. The hood looked longer than an Escort.

That first trip, on the wrong side of the road, in the slush and snow, was a little hair raising. When I pulled away from the first stop the car threatened to swap ends; after some practice I found it easier to put the car in second for take-offs, and switch to Drive once in motion. I very soon discarded my plan to drive around and see all of the neighbourhood sights. I went slip-sliding straight back to the hotel.

Next morning I looked out of my second floor window to see it was still snowing. Directly below my room was my car, with half a metre of snow on it. So began what was to become my ritual until the thaw arrived in February; up before six, early breakfast, ten minutes to clear the car of snow and ice, arrive at the massive car park behind WHQ, walk down one of the covered walkways into the super heated building, walk along almost deserted corridors to my office, and start working. Outside it was still dark.

I really had nothing to do but work while I was in Detroit. One weekend I went with new friends to Chicago, and I accompanied another friend into downtown Detroit once to pay a utility bill and he scared the heck out of me by opening his cubby hole to get at his gun faster if needed. I also made friends with a German couple who stayed in the pretty university town of Ypsilanti and visited them some

Sundays. Other then that my world was five kilometers of Michigan Avenue with an office at one end and a hotel room at the other.

I had to work hard because if McKinnon wasn't satisfied he could stop my appointment, and I had already seen enough to know that he set his standards high.

The first job was to analyse the data and produce the report of findings and recommendations from the Brazil car clinic. McKinnon had me work directly with him on this assignment, allowing me to do everything first and then correcting me. In this way I learnt fast about sample relevance (I wanted to draw conclusions from data where the sample was too small), and specially the crisp, point form of reporting.

I started to meet and get to know my colleagues in market research. As I studied each form of research that we would be using in South Africa, McKinnon would introduce me to the head of that section and I would work with them for a time, reading their material and questioning them. There was an extensive library of studies done over many years, as well as academic texts.

There were just over 40 market researchers in WHQ. None of them had less than a master's degree and more than half of them held doctorate degrees.

This was exactly what I wanted to learn from market research and had spoken about in my discussion with Kingsley Amm months before. I began to get a feel for what you could and couldn't learn from advertising research, the use of groups, statistical relevance of sample sizes, the limitations of rational responses from consumers, telephone versus face-to-face interviews, costs of research, demographics, psychographics; the list is endless.

These are some highlights I recall of events outside WHQ, or are they lowlights?

I attended the 10-day sales meeting of the Ford Division as an observer (there were two automotive divisions, the other being Lincoln Mercury). Every 10 days the region managers from throughout the States would fly to Detroit to attend this meeting.

It was run by the General Manager of the division and sales and stock statistics of the company and the dealers were projected onto a massive screen and analysed. It was basically a very public performance review, and quite brutal at times. I knew Americans were obsessed with short term results but this short term?

I also had the opportunity to attend a styling research session. It was held in a large auditorium with about 100 customers in the audience marking their responses on questionnaires. On the stage they portrayed various styling ideas using full size car models. The models were made of clay, but you could never tell them from the real thing. The cars would revolve and the presenter would say, do you prefer this side or this? This headlight treatment or this? This C-pillar design or this?

Of course American cars have annual model year changes, so the designs can be freshened on a more regular basis. But I do not believe consumers can be used in car design in the manner I observed that day. Later I deal with this subject in a chapter on Mercedes-Benz design, where they do it very differently.

After six months in the America's I was very homesick and thrilled to see Mount Kilimijaro, as we came in to land at Nairobi. Never mind that I was more than 6000 kilometres from Port Elizabeth, I was home, in Africa.

Chapter 11.

My Africa.

"I was home in Africa" were the last words of the previous chapter. How strange is it for a white South African to make this statement?

I was born in East London in the Eastern Cape during the last days of the Second World War. My father worked in a foundry as a moulder, my mother was a shop assistant. My father's work was regarded as essential services to the war effort and he was not allowed to join the military. This was frustrating and humiliating to him; on one occasion a woman presented him with a white feather of cowardice when he and my mother were walking down Oxford Road. He went north to the Reef and worked for a while in the giant iron and steel works of Iscor, and then went further north to Rhodesia.

We arrived by train in Bulawayo in 1945 on the day I turned one. When I was seven we moved to a farm west of the town. The farm was a vast tract of land which the municipality had purchased for a future black housing development. On it was an old home built in the style of the day with a verandah made of Rhodesian teak running around it on three sides.

So I became a child of the soil. I was a day scholar and would get home around three in the afternoon, put on a pair of takkies and go walking in the bush with my pellet gun and dogs. I find it hard to conjure up a mental image of this child walking out alone almost every day but the land is easily remembered; the animal paths I walked along, the rocky outcrop north of the homestead, the grassland to the south with its white sandy soil pockmarked with the holes of the antbear.

This is a poem of a memory of a strange happening from that time;

It's not fun when you're young.

It's not fun when you're young
To go our shooting in the night.

Dark forms of the men ahead of you
Dark, dark night.

And the light without colour
From the miner's lights on their heads
And the torch in your hand.

You get so tired, keeping up
Stumbling in the long, long grass.

Then a squeak, only you hear
In the grass, pinned by your light
A baby hare, all eyes and long legs.

He shivers in your hand but does not struggle
And in your shirt, in that warm dark place
He is so quiet.

You have another place for him
With your new rabbit
Your soft, grey and white rabbit.

In the morning
You rush to see them.

And he is gone, dead, eaten by the rabbit
The soft, grey and white rabbit
It's not fun when you're young.

My family moved back to South Africa in 1963 and I went back with them. It was the end of my final school year and the following year I enrolled at Rhodes University in Grahamstown.

In Rhodesia I felt I belonged and it was a shock to find that I was an outsider in South Africa; the land was claimed by the white Afrikaner and they told you so. Sadly they were setting themselves up for the tremendous alienation they feel today when the land is claimed by the black South Africans. And they also tell you so.

The English-speaking white in South Africa has for a very long time been disenfranchised. And it happens not only in our own country but also when travelling overseas. When I lived in Detroit I often encountered incredulity that I was white and that I regarded myself as an African, as if I had no right to such an assertion. I found that rich coming from a nation in which the majority of people descended from immigrants who arrived in the late 19th and early 20th century.

My first ancestor arrived in South Africa fully 50 years earlier than the great influx of Europeans into America, at a time when most of the black immigrants were still making their way down the east coast; yet her effort and sacrifice does not give me a birthright in the eyes of many of my countrymen. She arrived with what has become known as the 1840 German Settlers; her husband was a German mercenary who had fought for the British in the Crimean War, she was an English girl from Colchester.

Maybe this poem about her sets the record straight. I wrote it sitting in a tiny bar in Tofu, Mozambique, overlooking one of the most beautiful beaches.

My African ancestor.

I imagine she was a strong girl
My ancestor
She had to be
For the things that lay ahead.

I imagine she was excited
About the adventure with her German
Perhaps other girls from her village in Essex
Were also going.

I'm sure they had no past
No prospect for an easy future
Why not a life on the shores of a new land
With her mercenary soldier.

They were not to know the grand plan
The rough fighters hired for aspiration in Crimea
Now a nuisance
Better employed as a buffer in Africa.

The excitement would not have lasted long
I cannot imagine the fear and nausea and smells
Of dozens of settlers
In those small wooden shells.

Then the life in the town
Surrounded by hills
In a world of strange people and animals
But already an ally growing in her womb.

Her husband did not last long
Not for him the duty of birth
Not for him
Trained to deal in death.

And now the amazing part
The journey on foot with her child
In those rude times
To the garrison on the Buffalo River.

What was that journey like in the 1840's
A journey which takes me
Just over an hour today
On the smooth national roads.

No roads for her
The steep descents to the wide Fish River
Dense shrub and the sounds of lion and jackal in the night
Ever-present threat of Xhosa raiding parties.

In the town of soldiers she finds her security
A farrier named Norris
Perhaps not as exciting as her German
But a base from which to grow her family.

There are no chronicles for this story
I need my imagination
To give colour
to my birth as an African.

My daughter Susan was bemoaning the loss of many friends immigrating elsewhere mainly because of the fear of violence. She tells them "No-one ever came to South Africa because it is safe".

It reminded me of the extraordinary achievements of the early pioneers to this country, the black nations progressing down the east coast, the whites heading out from their beachhead in the Cape. The only true indigenous people, the San, retreated before this influx of more powerful and numerous people, eventually settling in the great Kalahari desert.

I wrote a tongue-in-cheek newspaper ad of these events, and this is an extract;

"The black folks struggled down the east coast of the continent, squabbling amongst each other, and encountering natural obstacles and wild animals.

The white folks landed in the Cape and struggled east,

squabbling amongst each other, and encountering natural obstacles and wild animals.

In the nineteenth century they met in the eastern Cape.

Two centuries of conflict followed during which the original folks were shoved off to the north west corner of the land".

For a wonderful few years it seemed that South Africans would overcome the prejudices of the past. Nelson Mandela was released from prison in the 90's and became president after a most inspiring vote for democracy in 1994. Mr Mandela embraced all the citizens of his country and gave hope for a future free of the strife of the past.

Sadly lesser men are now in charge and race has once more become a reason for divisiveness.

Fortunately the core of my love for Africa is not defined by people or countries. Early in my life I developed a habit of solitude; it was something my parents worried about but they had no need to, I was merely in communication with the natural environment I found myself in.

The enduring images are of remote locations; the cry of the eagle in the kopjies, the cooling evening and squeak of bats, the dawn walks in desert and bushveld. I have developed a love for landscape photography as it takes me to those remote places at dawn and dusk, and my eye is attuned to the nuances of light and form.

How fortunate I was to be born an African.

CHAPTER 12.

New car buyer surveys.

The annual new car buyer surveys were the mainstay of the Ford South Africa market research programme.

While I was in Detroit I had prepared the proposal for that year's survey, which included survey design, questionnaire, sampling methodology, costs and so on, and had it approved by McKinnon.

The new car buyer survey measures the owner's experience with his or her new car, their demographics, their media habits, their leisure activities and their perceptions of other cars in the same class as the car they bought.

Much of the information that we obtained through the medium of buyer surveys in those days is now available through syndicated research in South Africa. The All Media and Product (Amps) survey, for example, measures the media habits of South Africans cross-referenced to product ownership and customer demographics, psychographics and behaviour; an outstanding survey and essential for media buying.

It is also now possible to see owner experience and image, and things gone wrong data in Synovate and J.D. Power annual surveys.

In the 1970's the new car buyer survey was the only source for this information and this is how we used it;

Customer rankings of car features were used to understand that model's strengths and weaknesses for incorporation into design and assembly changes, and as the basis of market and price positioning.

Rankings of other models in the class (image) again provided feedback into the design process but mostly helped to understand the marketing and advertising opportunities that came from those areas where our car was relatively strong, but was not perceived to be that way.

Customer problem areas duplicated the information we received from the warranty system but allowed us to understand our competitive standing and gave feedback on the dealer's handling of the problems.

Customer demographics, media habits and leisure activities helped us with media buying and promotional activities.

When I got back from Detroit my first priority was to commission the buyer survey, and I did that by stopping over in Johannesburg where our market research agency was located, before even returning home. Despite the homesickness, business came first.

So began a new chapter in my life. The buyer survey came out of the field and I spent days with the agency in Johannesburg, preferring to be close to the source to work through any anomalies that could not be explained and might be errors in data capture or some other glitch from the agency.

The writing of the report was always fun and a challenge. We wrote a detailed report, to be studied in depth by departments in marketing and in product planning, then a summary and finally a one-page executive summary.

The report and tables were sent to McKinnon for approval before being circulated within the local company and to Ford of Europe, where our high volume cars were designed. Presentations were made to the Directors and senior management, and to departments that could use the data.

Apart from the buyer surveys there were other small ad hoc surveys but I was waking up to an uneasy fact; there wasn't enough work.

My boss at the time was Gordon Wright, one of the old school brigade; a decent enough bloke, but he had a limited understanding of market research and no inclination to change that. I remember playing games to gain his attention; once I turned in an expense account after a trip to Johannesburg with a zero claim. No comment was elicited, I'd wasted my money!

I produced an analysis of the correlation between market share and customer experience as shown in the buyer surveys. I called it Rejecter Analysis and was pleased when McKinnon got rather excited about it.

It is always difficult, if not impossible, to isolate single influences on market share movement. Cars change, competitors change, prices change, economic conditions change and advertising changes, so which of these caused the market share to improve or deteriorate?

The correlation I found that had a consistent fit was product and build quality. The quality ratings of the Ford Cortina had consistently worsened, and so had its market share. My presentation to the directors elicited a mixed reaction, with the manufacturing people being defensive. No direct action came from that meeting but I like to think it was one of a combination of factors which led to Ford building a new assembly plant for Cortina.

If that finding on the importance of quality seems obvious, I have to explain that it is not always so. Today, one of the cars with the greatest number of product problems, the VW Citi Golf, is the second-best selling model in South Africa.

Just when I was becoming restless and frustrated, one of the best American marketing men I have met arrived in South Africa.

Chapter 13.

Jack Givens.

Jack Givens, the new marketing head of Ford South Africa, was a dandy.

Ruthlessly ambitious and a perfectionist to the point of obsession, but a dandy nevertheless.

His tall spare frame was always impeccably clothed, the jacket buttoned when he left his office, the tie precisely fixed and matched, and the hair always in place. He had some excesses which soon became office gossip, an example of which was that he decided the hair salons in Port Elizabeth were not suitable and traveled 900 kilometers to Johannesburg for regular haircuts.

His appearance and his habits fueled the dislike for those whose working life had become more difficult because of his demands and autocratic management style.

Not me.

I found him refreshing and challenging, and he was the first man in his position who understood the marketing game. He not only understood the theory, he had done the job; managed advertising agencies, used market research and developed price and product proposals.

I had previously had colleagues and direct superiors who I could learn from and with whom I could discuss the theory and practice of our work. For the first time the head of marketing was such a person, and the managers in between suddenly had to up their game.

Within a short time Jack had me reporting directly to him and was using me as a sounding board on a variety of subjects. But not before two incidents in which I had to challenge him.

The first was his misconception of the image of Ford in South Africa. At that time Ford was still a force in the US with more than 20% of the market; the top foreign competition was VW and the Japanese were still regarded as upstarts. Surely it was the same in South Africa?

Such notions would result in poor decision making.

I arranged a group discussion of Cortina and competitor make owners in the offices of our research agency in Johannesburg. The customers were English- speakers from the East Rand, an area renowned for strong men with strong opinions. Jack and I watched through a two-way mirror. He had never heard Ford cars described in such a fashion!

We could discuss image in an objective manner after that and he became a driver for improved product quality and advertising focusing on our known strengths.

The second was entirely trivial, but important to him because it concerned taste in a television commercial. One of our two agencies had developed a TV commercial for the Ford Granada. As market research manager I was usually involved, this time because they needed my support with Jack.

The opening shot showed the car sweeping around a corner emerging from a sunspot. I knew Jack would not approve the sunspot but the commercial was drab without it. We prepared the defences; first we arranged to have an attractive woman editor on the monitor so that he would moderate his behaviour, and second I waxed lyrical about the mystical effects of that sunspot.

He knew what I was doing and he liked me for doing it. This was the cut and thrust that he thrived on. We got our approval on the commercial.

Givens always had an eye on what the South African experience could do for his career when he returned to the US. It was his least endearing quality and it was about to cause him to get egg on his face.

We had two advertising agencies. The oldest was JWT, based in Johannesburg, and the youngest was situated in Cape Town. Both of them kept contact offices in Port Elizabeth. As I argue several times in this book I don't believe competition between agencies improves the advertising, on the contrary it induces unproductive fear and cost. One agency means you have more spending power and that usually results in the agency giving you the best resources. When it falls down you manage it.

Jack held the same belief and he was itching to fire one of the two agencies. His motivation was OK to a point, but he really wanted firing an agency on his CV. It was not something he would get experience of in the US.

JWT was doing the worst job of the two and he decided to go for them. Unfortunately for him they had long standing relations with senior managers in Sales and Marketing and they were tipped off.

Jack asked me to go with him on this heroic adventure.

JWT had magnificent offices in one of the highrise buildings in downtown Johannesburg. When we exited the lift on their floor their Chairman was waiting for us in their impressive lobby. He said; "Jack, excuse me for not being polite, but I don't think you will want to meet under these circumstances. After much soul searching we have decided to resign the Ford account".

We got back in the lift and went back to Port Elizabeth.

I had planned my next move.

I wanted to get into sales. Like my initial motivation to understand market research so that I understood customer motivation, I had to have sales experience to understand dealer motivation. Without understanding the dealer you can never maximize your marketing effort to the consumer. The dealer was the instrument to deliver the promise of the brand.

It was interesting to me that Ford of Britain, one of the slickest marketing operations in the Ford world (at one stage they had three models in the top five sellers), insisted that their marketing managers had field experience. Even relatively senior sales and marketing managers were made to spend time serving dealers at jobs ranked considerably lower than the ones they held. When they returned to their original jobs they were better qualified, knowing what you could do with that difficult instrument, the dealer.

Unfortunately the jobs that I had done typecast me as a staff man in the eyes of George Simpson the Vehicle Sales Manager. He wanted relationship men in the field and he never saw me in that light, even when I became successful under his leadership.

Simpson had recently transferred to automotive sales after running a highly successful Tractor operation in South Africa.

At that time Ford tractors were the dominant brand and the organization to back the dealers was small and focused and extremely well-liked by dealers. George came with a strong power base among dealers, specially rural dealers.

Jack paid me back for my support and persuaded Simpson to give me a chance as a District Manager in the Johannesburg regional office.

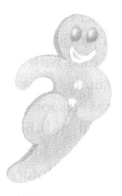

CHAPTER 14.

Regional Office.

If anything illustrated the fact the Ford was the training ground for the South African industry, it was the composition of the Transvaal/Free State Regional Office.

I arrived to take the place of Errol Richardson who was returning to Port Elizabeth to take up a fleet sales position.

Errol was later to head up the Toyota division of McCarthy Motors and spearheaded the growth of the group into overseas markets. He was one of a small cadre of top McCarthy managers who could have been promoted to their MD position, but McCarthy inexplicably preferred to fill this position with managers who had excelled in the wholesale side of the business.

The senior District Manager in the region office was Barry Hastings who dealt with the Eriksens and Grosvenor groups in Johannesburg.

Barry became the head of the Mercedes-Benz dealers owned by the Barlows Group. He and I served together on the DaimlerChrysler dealer council where he took the parts portfolio and achieved many concessions to improve dealer conditions. Barry sadly died with still much to achieve in his work and with his family.

Willie van Wyk was responsible for the dealers in Pretoria, western Transvaal and the East Rand. Willie had a successful career with Ford before joining Delta, the local group that ran the General Motors operation when they left the country. Willie became Managing Director of Delta Motor Company, and was able to retire quite young when they sold the company back to GM. Rumour has it he drives a Mercedes-Benz today!

In the Free State we had Arthur Mutlow. Arthur lived in the center of his district, Bloemfontein, and traveled the 300 kilometers every Friday to attend our weekly meetings. He later held positions with a number of motor manufacturers including Sales and Marketing Director at Nissan.

What a group of tigers!

I was to be responsible for the dealers in the northern and eastern Transvaal, the West Rand and Swaziland. In all there were over 20 dealers, and one group, Eastvaal Ford, was my biggest dealer with branches in Witbank, Middelburg, Ermelo, Nelspruit and Phalaborwa. I chose to live in Irene, just south of Pretoria for a quick start to the east and north.

Trying to put the lid on this young bunch was another of the old school brigade, Noel Trevett. I never saw much of Noel; he never visited any of my dealers at their premises, choosing, probably correctly, to use his influence with the big groups.

The only time he did go with me on a dealer visit was to the order take with Eastvaal Ford at their head office in

Johannesburg. And it was to prove an embarrassment to me, and a good illustration of the old and new methods.

I prepared myself well for monthly order takes, studying area penetration reports which told me how well the dealer was doing in the various segments of his own market area. Those reports showed me that the small van segment was non-existent in the rural towns; it was strictly a vehicle with appeal in the cities. As a result I had stopped trying to sell Escort Vans to Eastvaal.

When I skipped the section on Escort Van I received a mighty kick under the table from Noel. He berated Harry Shill, the MD of Eastvaal for not ordering vans and they argued backwards and forwards until Noel won the battle and Harry ordered a van for two of his branches. But he did not win the war because those vans became dead stock and stopped the order for vehicles which could have sold.

Noel lunched on that story for longer than I thought funny. His story did not include the bad ending!

The routine in the region office was to spend time visiting dealers from Monday to Thursday. Friday we were required to be in the office to report the results of our activities, and plan for the following week.

Dominating our work was the monthly order take cycle. We were required to do a physical order take with each dealer every month. The cycle took around ten working days, including consolidation on a regional and national basis. Unsold stock required us to have another crack at the dealers, this time on the telephone as time was short.

Ford had the flexibility at that time to even change the 30-day production programme providing parts stock was in the country. Manufacturing were always asked if they could produce 30 more of this model, or 25 less of that model.

That put pressure on the assembly plants, the supply people and the guys at the end of the line, us.

We all sang the tune to the dance of the market.

CHAPTER 15.

Working with dealers.

The Sales Manager at Eastvaal Ford in Middelburg could have been the model for a cartoon of a used car salesman. He was an Englishman, in a place where very few spoke English, (even his live-in girlfriend was Afrikaans speaking) he had a broad accent, was short, strong, energetic and profane.

Stan ran his large operation (they sold over 200 new and used vehicles a month) with an iron fist and a few hard rules. For example the used warranty lasted until the car left the lot and heaven help a salesperson who took the customer's side.

I loved to be in Middelburg because I learnt so much about car salesmanship and management from Stan, although the parts I remember tend to be of the kind that is not encouraged today.

I remember a salesman coming into his office and saying his customer wanted to buy a Cortina station wagon, but not the green one they had in stock. He was told to sit the lady down with a cup of tea, take the car around the back and have a radio fitted, then offer it to the customer with a free radio. She bought the green car.

I had some eccentric dealers.

The dealer in the beautiful town of Louis Trichardt would only do the order take with me on the golf course. As a result, and that was his intention, I got to know him quite well and often visited his magnificent home in the mountains. One evening Frank told me about his ranches across the border in Rhodesia, and how he smuggled cattle across the Limpopo River when money was tight.

The dealer in Messina often complained that I didn't stay at the hotel he owned in the town, but it was too hot for me. One evening after staying for a few drinks, I was driving back to my hotel in the mountains above Louis Trichardt when the airconditioner in my Granada froze because it could not handle the outside temperature.

I was fortunate to have dealers situated in some of the most scenic parts of the world, let alone South Africa. One such place was Lydenburg, where the dealership, McGee and Kie was situated outside town on the road leading to the Long Tom pass and Sabie.

But there was no point visiting because Bob always made sure to be away when I came, even when I made an appointment. I worked it out in the end; he just did not like confrontation and I had to fax the order take to him and he would send it back with a ridiculously inadequate order after much begging.

The dealer in Bronkhorstspruit was really only interested in tractors. The town is situated in the maize belt and every year they would buy up used tractors in the Transvaal and Free State and prepare them for sale when the season came.

Their yard was always full of perhaps more than 100 tractors in varying stages of repair.

The owner, Mr. Lazarus (his son features in a later chapter on performance groups), who sat on the showroom floor, was delighted when I visited him once as he had received a gift of an ashtray from Ford, the first free thing he had ever received, he told me. The next time I visited he was not as happy; an invoice had arrived for the ashtray!

I was doing plenty of traveling. Car policy at the time dictated that the car had to be replaced every 10 000 kilometers and that meant every two months or less for me. The district managers had to sell their used cars to a dealer, who in turn would be sent the replacement car to be prepped.

One such replacement taught me that there is a customer for every car.

At that time we were going through an idiotic experiment that a car could be built in any colour and with any option available. My new car (we never had a choice, we were sent the oldest cars in the stockyards in Port Elizabeth) was a Cortina 3000 LDO, the LDO standing for Luxury Décor Option. Nothing matched; it was a yellow car, with a tobacco coloured vinyl roof and grey cloth interior. I was relieved when Fletcher's Ford Sales in Roodepoort offered to buy it. They sold it within half an hour of putting it on display, before I even finished my visit with them that day.

I did not know the term at the time but I was applying best practices. If you kept your eyes open and asked questions you could always find the solution for one dealer's problems in the practice of another dealer. This was the most exciting part of my job, and I just loved everything about the job of being a district manager working with dealers.

I was able to help Fletchers Ford Sales in two ways, one

of which was not comfortable. The owner Bob Fletcher was a recluse. When he did visit his business he repaired immediately to his office where he sat in the dark, with a low lamp to illuminate what he was reading. He had two managers of equal standing and he could not choose between them for the dealer principal's job, or if he could he preferred to let someone else do the dirty work on the candidate who lost out.

Mr. Fletcher asked Ford for recommendations on his management structure, which meant I had to do the choosing between the two candidates.

Willie Haas became the dealer principal and the dealership flourished under the management of one person. Willie had marketing flair, but asked me to help with his advertising. Their building had a clock tower on it and I suggested they use this as a device in all their ads (I even drew the tower for them!)

Together with this symbol, which became well known, Willie came up with the strategy of advertising cars for sale at a cost plus price. Consumers then, and now, believe dealers have high mark-ups on cars and they flocked to buy cars at cost plus 10%, at which price the dealer made more profit than before. I never understood why other dealers did not follow Willie's cost plus strategy because his success was obvious for all to see.

The success I felt I was having with my dealers was not changing the opinions of either Noel or George Simpson that I was a staff, not a line man.

Fortunately for me George decided to increase the heat on the 9 district managers in the country by putting up an honours board outside the executive dining room in Ford House in Port Elizabeth. The board had a big picture of the best district manager of the month, and then smaller pictures of the rest in descending order. Best was measured in retail sales to target.

I soon worked out that only the best and the worst district manager would get noticed. If I cruised every second month coming around half way on the board, and then put in a big effort to have all sales reported by my dealers in the alternative month, I might actually get my managers to acknowledge that I was OK at the job.

In the last eight months I worked in the field I was on top of that board 3 times and second once. The rest of the time I placed in the middle.

Ironically my next move was to do more than the honours board to change opinion. I joined Eastvaal Ford.

CHAPTER 16.

First (very short) time as a dealer.

Eastvaal Ford was owned by the Brozin family and managed by Harry Shill, who I think owned shares in the business.

They were traders and operators and had little time for the fancy trappings of large corporations. Harry often bragged that he had once traded a donkey and cart on a used car.

They also moved fast on threats, and when the war in Mozambique escalated, and there were fears of intrusions on South Africa's eastern borders they sold the dealerships they perceived to be vulnerable. Harry sold up and went to settle in New Orleans where he bought a hotel.

So it was somewhat surprising that they decided to hire someone to put procedures and standards into their motor dealerships.

The person they hired was Bill Bayford. Bill had been a fighter pilot, and after the war he joined Ford and had worked his way through the ranks to the position of top job in the tractor operation of the company. He was a precise and disciplined man of high integrity and with compassion for the honest grafter; not the ideal temperament and value system for his new bosses.

I had worked with both Bill and Harry on problems with their dealerships and they obviously liked what I had to say and offered me a job.

I think I accepted the job for two reasons. One was my usual desire to do something new and different, but which advanced my marketing expertise; the same motivation that had driven me from industrial relations to market planning, to market research, and into sales. The second was a bad reason to leave; I wanted to prove my detractors wrong.

Whatever my motivation, I soon saw that I would be unable to work for Eastvaal Ford for too long. Two memories stand out of my short time with them.

Harry visited his dealers in a light aircraft owned by the company (in typical fashion of extracting maximum advantage from every situation, the pilot's idle time was taken up auditing used stock at the branches). There was no timetable, in fact the opposite, as visits were sometimes designed to surprise the managers. As there were also no cell phones in those days the branch manager found out we were there when the plane buzzed his building.

The manager of the Witbank branch had played provincial rugby as a lock. He was a large, fit, handsome and self-assured man in his early thirties. And then he had a nervous breakdown. I spent time standing in at the Witbank branch while they were finding a replacement and realized that this game is not as easy as it seems. There is a lot of pressure and particularly in his case as he had let things slide and lived in fear of being found out.

Two months after joining Eastvaal Ford, Jack Givens

phoned me and offered me a job as Advertising and Market Research Manager back in Port Elizabeth.

I never changed jobs for money but these fortuitous moves swelled the meager Cleary fortunes. I was earning R450 a month as a District Manager, went to Eastvaal Ford for R650 and was now returning to the fold at R1 000 a month!

Chapter 17.

Running an advertising department.

I love the advertising game, both as facilitator as an advertising manager in a large corporation and as a practitioner in a small way, writing my own ads when I became a dealer.

But I never got used to having to play the political game that was needed to ensure that outstanding work could find its way into the media without change that weakened it.

It is why advertising managers play games with their agencies, either not showing emotion and approval for the work spontaneously in case there should be a reversal, or being disloyal to all by siding with the agency behind closed doors, and criticizing them in front of company bosses.

I couldn't be one of those managers; I valued good advertising and the people who created it too highly.

That does not mean I won the battles, I lost plenty and each one left a little scar which meant I was never going to allow myself to stay in such a position for too long. The problem is that if you can't distinguish between good and bad advertising then you cannot see why small changes should not be made; I had to contend with that argument all the time.

The real downside is that eventually the agency plays the political game, produces the stuff they know will sell in the boardroom, even if it doesn't sell in the market place.

I remember a number of excellent campaigns that died in the boardroom.

The Ford Granada was a good car in its category, offering value, roominess, road holding and performance. It had been positioned as a luxury car of good quality, a positioning that could never fly against the German luxury cars.

I wanted to change the positioning and we did group discussions with owners to find what distinguished the car in their eyes. What we found struck a chord with me and with the agency. Granada had a very wide stance and was powerful when seen in your rearview mirror. Such a positioning enabled us to strengthen perceptions of roominess, performance and road holding, which were strengths we knew existed from our buyer surveys.

The agency's brilliant campaign had the headline "Move over for Ford's big strong Granada".

It died because one of the senior sales and marketing managers said it was a risk that the message would mean the car had poor fuel consumption. I could not resuscitate it, even when I wasted the company's money producing some research which showed it did not have those connotations.

We ran out one of the Cortina models with a nostalgia theme. This was an approach used very successfully by VW and we were convinced that Cortina had enough heritage to carry the approach. The agency employed one of the best illustrators in the country to develop the visual, incorporating all of the previous models, as well as the Cortina GT racing models and well-known drivers who made their name in that car.

We could make a softer approach as a prelude to the imminent launch of the new model because it looked like we would have a smooth run out. But then George Simpson lost confidence that the run out would be that smooth and forced us to place a flash across the ad announcing specials on certain models. Another camel.

It seems that I have a memory of those days that selects the bad moments, and it is a great pity that I remember so vividly the failures and not the successes. I rectified this when I was facilitating advertising for Mercedes-Benz years later and could approve the work myself (see chapter headed Advertising Mercedes-Benz).

One of the successes was Lew Slade who joined me to do market research. Lew and his wife Judy had come to South Africa to settle from England. He was brought out as a graduate trainee with one of the retail chain stores and was not enjoying that industry as much as he had hoped. It was my and Ford's good fortune and I really enjoyed helping him to learn the market research and advertising game, and he in turn stimulated me with fresh approaches.

Lew went on to be the chairman of one of the biggest advertising agencies in South Africa and made enough money to retire early.

A few years ago we were holidaying with Cathy's sister and her husband at Cape St. Francis, and right next to us, on the canal, was the home of Lew and Judy Slade. They had retired there several years earlier and made a wonderful life for themselves, Lew did woodwork in his garage and was the lay preacher of a small church they had started with friends.

He told me how much reward he received from composing his sermons.

At least one of my friends had used the motor industry as a stepping stone to a rich and satisfying life.

CHAPTER 18

The last Cortina.

I had done 360 degrees in marketing and ended up back where I started, this time managing the functions. As Car Marketing manager I was responsible for marketing strategy and sales planning, and as the resident market research expert that function also trailed along behind me.

It was exciting work, specially being able to see sales planning in a different light after my experience as a district manager selling the vehicles to the dealers. We were now the department that collated the results of the order take and went to the board every month with our requests for changes to the production plan.

There was a very big job that needed to be done and it needed to be done fast; we had to change the Cortina model line-up for the Mark IV version which was due for launch in South Africa within a year.

The Cortina was our most important car but its model line-up was a marketing and logistical nightmare. The car came in four engine versions, each of which could be specified with three trim and specification lines. The top engine could also have a fourth trim option. In all there were 12 models possible. And that was excluding automatic transmission models and station wagons.

We started with the engines, which we knew would be difficult to change because they were manufactured locally and an important part of our local content strategy which was measured by weight in those days.

The bottom of the range engine, the Kent engine, was reasonably competitive in terms of power and fuel consumption and could be retained in 1,6l form for Cortina.

The problem lay in our Essex V-engine range which was manufactured in 4 and 6-cylinder versions and in 2,0l, 2,5l and 3,0l capacities, all of which were then offered in the run out model. The V4 engine was a disaster. Inherently unbalanced it required a massive crankshaft to remove the worst of the vibration. It had poor fuel consumption and the power delivery came high in the torque curve.

The 2,5l V6 engine was also curiously less efficient than its 3,0l brother. But this was less of a problem because we did not believe we needed two 6-cylinder versions. There was a better fuel-injected 6-clinder engine available out of Ford's Cologne plant but the 3,0l V6 was a well known and loved engine at that time. An earlier advertising campaign had labeled the engine "Big Six" and buyers liked that so much that the car was badged that way on the front fenders.

The big headache was what to do for the midrange engine. Your midrange car is always the most important for profitability, because the cheapest versions of most models don't make money and you need to attract customers to the next car up the price range which usually has a reasonable profit margin.

If we continued with the Essex V4 we would not only have an uncompetitive model, but buyers would prefer the 1,6l Kent model which would damage profitability.

The answer lay in the German 2,0l OHC in-line 4-cylinder engine which would have to be imported and local content made up elsewhere. We would have to restrict volumes on this engine until the local content shortfall was made up.

We turned our attention to the trim versions. In the present model you could get your 1,6l Cortina in "L", "GL" and "GLS" versions. That made no sense to the consumer and you could see it in the sales. Your 1,6l buyer could not afford the more expensive trim versions. Similarly, the buyer of the 3,0l version did not want a low line level of trim and features.

Our strategy with the low and mid range models was easy; the 1,6l car would come with "L" trim only (but we made sure this was a better level of specification than the equivalent trim level in the run out model), and the 2,0l would only be available with "GL" levels of trim and specification.

For the 3,0l engine we wanted to market two different cars, a luxury and a sports version. The luxury version would be a conservative car with every feature available, such as cruise control, to be fitted standard. This version was to be badged "GLE".

The sports version had to be visually exciting both on the exterior and interior of the car and we found enough hardware in the Ford world to see that we could differentiate this model very well. We toyed with names and eventually copied Ford of Britain who had come out with a "XR" designation on an Escort. We suggested "XR6" which kept the 6-cylinder nomenclature alive.

We worked day and night in Car Marketing to get this strategy completed with model line-up, specification, volumes and prices. Very few people knew that such a radical change was to be proposed and we gave much thought to the reaction it would receive.

We knew manufacturing would love the reduced model line-up but worry about losing engine volume in their plant, and worry about sourcing extra local content in a very short time.

Key to approval was Product Development which would have the most work, firstly in their product planning department which would have to calculate investment and profit, and would have to obtain approval from Ford of Europe for the strategy and to use the "XR6" designation, and in their engineering departments which would have to release the new and changed parts affected, and provide specifications and drawings for parts which would be made locally, and finally in their testing department which would have to run an accelerated programme for the new engine and for a sports suspension for the "XR6" model.

Surprisingly the most opposition came from sales and marketing who were still in the mode of offering everything to the consumer and saw the rationalized model line up as a volume risk. But I knew we were right and insisted that the proposal go to the board of directors.

The day of the presentation to the directors was a nervous one. I needn't have worried. Derrick Morris, the Product Development Director was enthused by the possibilities, as was Doug Kitterman the Managing Director, and most of the discussion was about how we were going to get the job done in the extremely short time available.

Eventually Derrick Morris said to Kitterman "there's only one way I can get this job done in time Doug, Pete's got to transfer to product planning".

So I began a new career which was to take me away from sales and marketing for nearly four years, and from South Africa for two of those years.

CHAPTER 19.

Lessons in humility.

There were a few times in my career when I ran into a brick wall, and Product Planning was probably the hardest of those walls.

The difficulty was a combination of the technical skills required to do the job, as well as the culture of the mostly British engineers in the Product Development office of Ford South Africa.

Product Planners regard themselves as the elite in the motor industry, mostly because of the pivotal role they play in the development of cars and trucks, but also because they are required to have technical, marketing and financial skills.

In deciding on a new model, or changes to an existing model, a motor company needs to evaluate the sales volumes and prices, estimate the investment required to develop and assemble the model, estimate timing and ultimately do a profit forecast.

And the product planners are the guys who pull that all together from an investigation they initiate and control, receiving information from engineering, manufacturing and marketing, and developing a proposal to the board with the assistance of the project planners in finance.

I can tell you from experience it is not easy. The job is made harder by engineers who drag their heels if they don't believe in the change, and by manufacturing who see the opportunity to rebuild sections of their plant every time a new model comes along. There is also the conflict with marketing who might want a product where the need is not backed up by empirical or research data, or the converse, where the planners identify a need which marketing does not believe is required.

When I started to get on top of the technical aspects of the job it became fascinating but first I had to learn to live with and understand the culture if I was to get the co-operation of my engineering colleagues.

There are always these little tests you are subjected to when you come from another department. I was the guy who had turned their world upside down by asking them to do the impossible in terms of the new Cortina, and they resented that; even though the good ones among them knew the late changes would improve the product. As a rule engineers don't like marketing people anyway.

My first test was administered by Bernie Marriner.

Bernie was the Competitions Manager who prepared and ran the outstanding Escort BDA team in the South African rally championships. He had been a national motor cycle champion and was reputed to be a very good car driver; a new test engineer who had joined us from Jensen in the UK told me Bernie was the fastest man on gravel roads he had ever driven with, but only for a short distance because Bernie got bored quickly.

I was walking through the development workshop when Bernie loudly called me over; "Hey Pete, I'm taking this car out for a run, want to come with me?" I sensed the immediate interest of everyone within earshot, and knew this was a set-up. A refusal on my part would have confirmed their worst opinions.

They could not have devised a crueler test because I hate to put my life in the hands of someone else, specially someone who got bored at 200 kph on gravel roads!

When I got into the car I saw that Bernie had not fastened his harness so I decided to tough it out as well, my first mistake because although those special seats are form hugging I was being thrown around and had to grip the underside of the seat frame to stop head butting the roof.

Through the public roads Bernie was all decorum, and then we hit the gravel, down a long straight. I could see quite a sharp bend at the end but Marriner kept accelerating. In those days of rear-wheel drive cars the quickest way to corner was a power slide but I had never experienced such a thing. So when the car suddenly went sideways at around 160 kph I said goodbye to my family and loved ones!

Fortunately I never screamed or begged him to stop so I guess I passed the test. Certainly Bernie regarded me as his pal from then on, a rare honour I was told.

The Product Planning Manager at the time was Keith Butler-Wheelhouse, but he was already making plans for his next move. Derrick Morris was Product Development Director. I was to come to know Derrick well and always liked and respected him, and he kept a special watch over me. Derrick unfortunately could not control his emotions and he often let himself down, a great pity because he was an outstanding engineer and manager.

They created a new job for me called Advanced Planning Manager, meaning I would handle the big projects still some way into the future, and of course I had to complete the Cortina planning first.

My biggest contribution in the short time I was in that position was to try to create order out of the chaotic nature of the planning process. I only did that because I did not understand the process myself and needed to break it down into its component parts to understand who interacted with whom, for what information and in what time frame. Everyone benefited from the structure I developed, even those who had worked in the loose regime that existed before.

Derrick had plans for me. He wanted me to be his product planning manager but first he thought I needed to work in Ford of Europe.

Chapter 20.

Ford of Europe.

On dark winter mornings the Engineering Centre in Dunton, England was lit up like a space mother ship. I was coming from Chelmsford on a narrow secondary road through dark farmlands and there it was, every morning, seen from the crest of a hill to the north west.

And in winter sometimes I did not see the sun the whole day. My office was windowless, in the middle of the smaller building which housed the brass and product planning; we took an underground tunnel to the canteen in the big building and emerged onto the freezing parking lot after sunset.

I had the impressive title of Product Liaison Manager, Ford Asia Pacific and Latin America. It meant I was the messenger boy. If anybody from the affiliate companies in the regions in my title wanted product or engineering information, and did not know who to ask, they asked me. And how was I to know?

In an ironical twist of fate my boss was Spence Sterling, located in Melbourne, where he was Director of Product

Development for Ford Asia Pacific. The time difference meant I had to get to the office early on a Friday morning so that he could talk on the phone to me before leaving the office for the weekend.

There was a real part to the job as well. When Ford of Europe approved a product which included export of vehicles or components to other countries, the proposals of the other countries had to be included in the approval process. I was the representative of those other countries and had to write their proposals into the main board documents. I was euphemistically called ROW; Rest of the World.

The product planners working in Ford of Europe were an impressive bunch. Firstly they had an international flavour, but with the emphasis on Europe. Ford of Europe was an amalgamation of Ford of Britain and Ford of Germany, brought together to stop the expensive business of designing cars in both countries.

I was there shortly after the amalgamation and the process was still clumsy. Car exteriors and suspensions were designed in Cologne, interiors and drive trains were designed in Dunton. German and English designers and engineers had to co-operate, and they also had to design for other national characteristics, soft ride for the French, handling the priority for the Germans. The company owned a fleet of BA 111's which flew out of Stansted airport to make it convenient for the two sides to talk to one another.

Being a stranger from a neutral country both sides used me to vent their opinion of the incompetence and maddening idiosyncrasies of their colleagues on the other side of the North Sea.

Secondly the product planners were highly qualified academically and had a wide range of interests. The guy occupying the office next to mine was French. We both drove Fiesta's, mine had a sport suspension. He asked that we swap cars one weekend. The radio pre-select had six stations; his were set to radio stations in four different languages.

Yet I was amused at the squabbling about conditions of employment. The Germans were the highest paid and the Brits complained that they went to Brighton for their annual holiday whilst their German counterparts went to Bali.

I loved the vibe in product planning and enjoyed myself immensely and learnt much when I had to do ROW submissions. But in a way, the other side of my job was even more interesting. Here are two of the projects I became involved in;

I arrived at my office late one afternoon to find three large Argentineans. I had a moments pre-warning from my secretary who explained that there were these men who had no appointment and she thought it better to seat them in my office.

After moments of awkwardness I eventually got the story from the one who spoke the best English; they were engineers from Ford Argentina and they were co-operating with a study being done by the Argentinean government, to determine why car prices were so high in their country. Like countries everywhere they could not accept that their local content programmes and duty structures were at fault.

Those engineers had to get the costs of producing parts in Europe, and to do so they had to visit the plants in which the parts were made.

At some point my secretary interrupted to say she could not find them a hotel room in London. We found them digs close to the village of Black Notley where I lived.

The next week I had to cancel everything I planned to

do and chaperone them to plants in Cologne and introduce them to people who could supply them with the information they needed. I never heard the outcome of the work they did. Their communication was as bad in going as it was in coming.

The other project was much more interesting and was to provide me with information which assisted me when I went to Australia the following year.

The countries in South East Asia wanted to have their own car plants. Ford met this challenge with an interesting strategy which unfortunately did not work. To get economies of scale they suggested to the countries concerned that they rather have a complementation programme so that higher volumes could be built in some countries of specific car parts for the whole region, and they could all have their own assembly plants.

Ford built an engine plant in Taiwan, a stamping plant in the Philippines and a gearbox plant in New Zealand. All three countries did not have the market to support such an expensive factory on their own. It didn't work; ultimately most of those countries got greedy and wanted it all; the New Zealanders decided motor car assembly could best be done elsewhere and dumped their fledgling industry.

I got involved because we had to fill the Philippines stamping plant with work. They were able to get orders for panels for cars out of production, but the volumes for service parts were low and that creates inefficiency in a stamping plant because of the idle time when stamping dies need to be changed. They needed just one part of a high volume product in current production in Europe. The Europeans were understandably not interested; all they needed was for production to be halted because a part did not arrive from the other side of the world.

In my effort to persuade someone to accept this corporate responsibility I was directed to visit a number of European plants. Eventually a visit to the Cortina plant in Genk, Belgium paid dividends. We were to be given a trial at producing the rear floor pan for Cortina at volumes which would take up a third of our production capacity in our plant.

The contract was finally granted, but not before we had to solve a packing problem; the first samples arrived rusted because water vapour had entered the packaging; the parts had to be sealed.

There was an unexpected benefit to my travels to Cologne; I discovered the cathedral. I never liked the fussiness of the exterior architecture but the awesome height and space standing in the middle of Cologne Cathedral is a spiritual experience like no other. I never missed a visit on my frequent overnight stays in that city.

CHAPTER 21

The North Atlantic divide.

I was fascinated by the difference between the American and British orientation; the specialist versus the generalist.

When I had lived in Detroit, studying market research, it had struck me how narrow the researcher's jobs were. In South Africa I had to do all aspects of the market research as I was the only researcher; analyzing the problem, determining the best approach, designing the questionnaire, briefing the agency, analyzing the results, reporting back, providing solutions and follow-up.

The people in Detroit specialized in only one or two of those branches, most of them did not even get to meet the people who had the problem for which the research had been designed. Their level of expertise in a narrow field was unbelievable and wonderful to me when I was learning to understand market research; yet I wondered about job satisfaction.

Now I had an even better perspective, comparing the approach of British versus American product planners.

It seemed to be rooted in the education system. Ford was highly regarded as an employer in both America and Britain, both countries were enjoying success in the market in the 70's and it meant something to be a product planner for the company.

In America the qualification required was a mechanical or automotive engineering degree from MIT and an MBA from Harvard. The two senior product planners in Ford of Europe had master's degrees in the classics from Oxford.

The Americans were obsessed with specifications, the British/Europeans with social trends. Both frustrated the other.

I was to have a chance to see the differences of culture and business orientation between the Americans and the Japanese in my next job.

There was one thing, however, that we all had in common; we liked to discuss the excesses of our boss, Mr. Ford. Henry Ford liked to visit London and had a town house in the city. The town house was modified to be able to show Mr. Ford the latest designs of his European companies and that meant more floors were added to the house; downwards.

My colleagues sneaked me in there when they were supervising the delivery of some new designs to be displayed in his underground studio.

Mr. Ford visited the Engineering Centre once while I was stationed in Britain. He had been having meetings with Ford of Europe management in their headquarters in Brentwood, about six kilometres away. The road between the two, a narrow country lane, was seen to be a security risk and a helicopter was employed to carry him the short distance.

Did we really want to be like that? You bet.

Chapter 22.

Melbourne.

It should have been an adventure. There we were seated in the front row of the first class cabin, a young family with children aged four and two journeying from Britain to Australia.

It was a nightmare. The children had flu and could not equalize the pressure in their ears. They were in pain with every change of altitude. And in that 22-hour flight there were plenty of landings; in the Gulf, India, Singapore, Sydney and finally our destination Melbourne. When the plane changed crews, the new crew had clearly been told of this difficult family.

We arrived at our hotel in the early afternoon and crashed for 12 hours. Then we woke in the early hours of the morning, wide-eyed with nothing to do; except to go window shopping in the deserted streets of downtown Melbourne at 4 a.m. on a Sunday morning.

On Monday I reported for what was to be the hardest working assignment of my entire working life. I had been picked to be part of a task group to investigate purchasing a shareholding in Mazda.

Ford had been approached by the largest shareholders of Mazda, the Bank of Japan, to invest in the ailing motor company. Mazda had enjoyed early success after the rebuilding of their plants in Hiroshima after the Second World War, and had grown a reputation for innovative engineering. Unfortunately they had tied their fortunes to the rotary engine and not had the flexibility to get out of the hole the first fuel crisis dug for them and their thirsty engine.

I remember one of my best loved ads when I was living in Detroit had been for a Mazda rotary-engine car. The visual had a boy on a pogo stick bouncing along and then being passed by a Mazda. The song being sung had lyrics that said; "the piston engine goes boom-bo-de-boom-bo-de-boom, the Mazda rotary engine goes vroooom".

As I write this I wonder if some agency, somewhere in the world, didn't dig up that ad and use it as the inspiration for the current "Zoom-zoom" corporate campaign for Mazda cars.

The task group was constituted in Melbourne as the primary target for Mazda-sourced small cars was seen to be the markets of south-east Asia, Australasia and southern Africa; my old rest-of-the-world bunch. In most of these markets the European-sourced Escort had not been successful and the primary reason for failure was seen to be price; it was hoped a small car sourced from Mazda in Japan could correct this situation.

The task group comprised an odd assortment from around the Ford world. The task leader was an American, and very well chosen; his drive to complete the assignment timeously and with an extremely high standard of analysis and presentation was balanced with a rare diplomacy. He was brilliant with the Japanese and with the task team members who toiled willingly for him.

The only Australian was not really an Australian; he was a Russian emigrant. I do Dave Fewchuk a disservice, he was born in Australia to Russian missionaries; his mother still visited Russia to smuggle bibles into the country when it was dangerous to do so. Dave was the only Australian from Ford Australia who accepted the assignment. I was amazed; if ever there was a fast track assignment this was it. We had Australian secretarial assistance.

Then there was Lyn Schroeder, another old mate from Rhodes University, on the other side of the world. Lyn deserves a paragraph or two; he was a brilliant sportsman who earned his colours for Border in four sports as a schoolboy. I played rugby with him at both under 20 and senior level. Lyn was from the Controller's office of Ford South Africa and was in demand throughout the world, specially at budget time.

He was once requested to assist Venezuela prepare their budget but could not get a visa for the country in South Africa; he was advised to travel to Rio de Janeiro and apply from there. Lyn spent three weeks in Rio, his only work task to phone daily and ask if the visa had arrived. The might of the travel company in Detroit could not accomplish the task; I reckon they were not fighting the Venezuelan authorities, they were fighting a lone South African on an unexpected paid holiday!

Amongst the others in the task team I remember a manufacturing engineering guy from England and a financial analyst from Malaysia, a girl of Chinese extraction with an MBA from Harvard. In all we had the people with the experience to evaluate every aspect of Mazda's operations.

I was the product planner in the group. It was my job to specify a Mazda small car which would best suit the markets we were studying and to have each of those markets provide me with product variances to suit their markets, and with volumes and prices.

It was, of course, impossible to forecast the likely sale of a vehicle based purely on its dimensions, features and performance. Mazda was present in the markets with varying success and understandably that performance had an influence on perception. The south-east Asian countries were strongly in favour, the Australians and South Africans were not.

The Australian's had had some success developing an Escort with a 2 litre engine, could they do this with a Mazda? In South Africa Escort did better than Mazda; that was to change in the 80's when the Mazda 323 became the best-selling car in the country.

And above it all I was conscious of the irony of studying just one model, and of making the Escort the scapegoat; in most of the south-east Asian countries where Escort was weak, the Cortina was exceptionally strong. A strong Escort replacement would take volume away from Cortina, a much more profitable car. Would the combination of a C class Mazda car and a C/D class Ford car be a better combination than the current two Ford entrants?

The south-east Asian countries had such unsophisticated marketing and planning people that they did not even understand the need to forecast the substitution rates. Their lack of understanding of our requirements became a major stumbling block for me; eventually I did pro-forma documents for them to complete the process, but even that was not enough. I ended up doing their plans and then cajoled and bullied them into accepting and signing them.

We toiled on, working 12 hour days, 6 days a week with the occasional Sundays thrown in. I lived in an apartment in Tourak, around 3 kilometers from our offices. I walked to work in the morning so that I could leave the car with my family. Much of the walk was along the edge of the park. It is one of the most beautiful parts of the world, not the normal image one has of Melbourne, the industrial city.

The walk in the morning really helped to restore my energy and optimism, but it was not easy for my family. They were in an unfamiliar place with an absent husband and father; we had few outings together and not one single day of leave that whole year. Such are the ambitions of youth.

CHAPTER 23.

Hiroshima.

Two tiny Japanese women, in traditional dress, were walking ahead of us down a long passage, leading us to the meeting room. Their custom did not allow them to turn their backs to us so they would scamper a few metres, turn and bow to ask our forgiveness, and then repeat the move. It was seriously cute.

A delegation of us was in Hiroshima for our first meetings with the Mazda people. Our trip to Hiroshima had been a delight, starting with a day flight out of Sydney to Hong Kong on Air New Zealand. The first class seats could be swiveled to face one another and we had played eight hours of serious poker.

In Hong Kong I took my first Star Ferry ride and we had a drink in the top bar of the Mandarin hotel, looking down at the amazing sight of Hong Kong harbour at night. The next day we flew to Tokyo and caught the bullet train to Hiroshima, another first for me. At Hiroshima station we were met by a tall stern-faced Japanese man, who was to be our interpreter for the period.

And now we were in the meeting room, and there was our stern-faced interpreter.

So began days of discussions and negotiations with our Japanese hosts. For the first few days they would only allow discussions in the one room even bringing our lunch into the room. We wanted to break into smaller groups to explore our many avenues of enquiry. We never knew why this was so because it was frustrating and inefficient; our best explanation was that they wanted to decide whether they would even go to the second level of discussion with us; they were testing us.

Eventually we could break into a group exploring the financial matters and a group exploring manufacturing and product issues. Stern-face stayed on as our interpreter.

When I reflect on that extraordinary visit I have more perspective on the difficulty they had in even having discussions with us. It was less than thirty years since their parent's generation, and even some of them, had been caught up in the horror of the first atomic bomb.

And here they were being asked to negotiate with an American company, the nation that performed the deed. You have to ask why the Bank of Japan forced this indignity upon them, or if European motor companies had rejected their overtures.

We could feel the hostility in the first days, and only once were we allowed to meet with them without the interpreters, and only on the last night with us did they entertain us and let their hair down.

The once they allowed a meeting was with me on a weekend. Our group was visiting the holy acre, the area directly below the bomb blast which had been left in its devastated state. I needed to spend time with the car that they were proposing for ROW markets. I had trouble explaining my need to them, the specifications and drawings were not enough, I wanted to see and touch, I wanted to be able to explain in detail my impressions to the markets studying introduction of this car.

Eventually they saw my point and allocated a studio to me in which stood the car and a Japanese engineer. I think his main role was to make sure I didn't pinch anything but in the end, probably through the boredom of watching me, he started to speak halting English, something stern-face had told me he could not do! And what an amazing story he told me; that his great love was pornography, and that his wife was not pleased and although their house was small she insisted he take his hobby to a small shed in the garden. It was too wild for me not to think it was planted to get a reaction.

More importantly I really liked the car and the quality of materials and assembly, and was going to be able to give a favourable report to my colleagues in the team and in the markets.

Hiroshima was just remarkable to the western eye, or at least to mine. It is a small city by Japanese standards, surrounded by round hills and situated on the Sea of Japan. When you stood in the centre of the city looking outwards to the ring of hills it was difficult to understand that some of those hills stood in the sea. The ring of hills was also the tragic reason the city was chosen as the site of the first atomic bomb, the hills contained the blast and made it even more effective.

Everything was so different. The narrow streets, the different materials used in the single-storey structures, the dress, the smells, the formal behaviour, the furtive glances, the market with fruit and vegetables as polished as a billiard ball, expensive fruits wrapped like Christmas presents. Wow. I so enjoyed our breaks from the discussions when we were able to wander through the streets and see the life of a small provincial Japanese city, far removed from the sophistication of Tokyo.

We had a delegation of engineers fly in from the US. It was headed by the Chief Engineer, Engines from the Ford Division. Our boss warned us that this guy could cause us problems in our developing relationship with our hosts. In the first meeting his attitude was overly aggressive and self-serving.

He explained that he would have the final say in this choice, and if Mazda did not have the level of engineering that met his standards he would veto a decision to buy a part of their company. He explained that recent research conducted by his department showed that there was only one design that maximized fuel consumption, a hemispherical combustion chamber. Did Mazda understand the importance of this discovery?

After much discussion our hosts understood his point and someone was dispatched from the room and returned soon after with engine designs. They showed a hemispherical combustion chamber. The designs were of a Mazda engine that had been in production for many years.

On the last night they took us out for a celebratory meal. We had got to know each other pretty well, despite the lack of conversation between us. We had watched them and they had watched us. I'm sure many of them also understood what we were saying but never let on. But finally we had great conversations going, mainly centered on the salutation to drink; Kampai.

When I left the restaurant I had a very light head and I walked for some time to try to get my wits back. It was snowing lightly but it wasn't cold, and it was a memory to cherish.

We eventually finished the mammoth body of work and presented our findings to Asia-Pacific management and obtained approval. Our project leader flew to Detroit to present to Mr. Ford and the main board of directors and phoned us to give us the good news; our proposals had been approved, Ford was to buy a 25% stake in Mazda.

When he came back he had more news; he was to head up a new division, Ford of Japan which was to be based in Tokyo to act as a liaison office with Mazda and to develop a dealer network for the sale of Ford products in Japan.

He invited me to be his marketing director but my family had just had enough. I often wondered if I would ever have worked in South Africa again if I had accepted his offer.

Chapter 24.

Product Planning in South Africa.

I returned to South Africa to take up the position of Product Planning Manager. It was another promotion and took me to the third highest tier of compensation in the Ford world.

I was thirty-four years of age, and it was my thirteenth job with Ford in eight years.

It was time to settle in and use my experience in the planning field. It was also time to pay back Derrick Morris who had provided me with the opportunities to work with Ford of Europe, and then had been prepared to release me for a further year to the Mazda study group.

We had some interesting work to do, specially in the field of pickups.

South Africans love pickups, as working, leisure and often as their primary vehicle. When I started working at Ford there was only a small population of small one-tonne pickups. The pickups on the market were both the larger American sourced F-Series, and its Chevrolet competitor, or Australian sourced Rancheros and El Caminos.

Soon, however, Toyota, Mazda, Isuzu and Nissan introduced one-tonne and half- tonne models and they became volume sellers eventually totally replacing the large American models and the expensive Australian models. Pickups had the advantage in the early years of their growing popularity because they fell outside the stringent parameters of the passenger car local content programme.

By the time the local content programme included pickups and they were subjected to higher investment and costs the market was entrenched. It was also becoming entrenched in terms of positioning in the minds of the consumer.

Later when we did a positioning study to help us with second generation Cortina pickup planning, we discovered strongly held views of where the customer perceived his pickup to be; on a continuum of car-like to truck-like, the middle position, the most desirable position, and the one that yielded the most sales, was held by the Toyota Hilux. At the extreme ends of the scale, not the ideal positioning, were the Cortina and the Nissan.

Isuzu held a desirable position close to the center with a skew towards truck-like. But they were the first to introduce diesel and 4x4 versions and for many years they kept the high ground in the sales of these versions; the diesel model also gave Isuzu a lead in the rural community, one which they have kept to this day, for example in the Eastern Cape.

Ford never had small pickups, and only has them today because of the Mazda connection. Ford South Africa became the first in the Ford world to design a pickup from a car platform. The Cortina was the ideal size, and the first pickup derived from it had a satisfactory record and we learnt much from it. The second generation model contained many features which overcame the weaknesses of the pioneer model; the main one was headroom because the rails to support the box structure and rear suspension protruded into the cabin under the seats, therefore raising the position of the seats.

This also became one of many arguments with Brian Pitt, when he was still Finance Director; our investigation showed that we could not use the roof from the sedan; we had to have a higher roof and revised front door design to make it work. Pitt balked at the investment in tooling and extra parts costs which we said could not be recovered in pricing. Eventually we fudged the numbers to show an increase in sales from the feature; something I hated to do because it was blatant rubbish.

We also repositioned the second generation pickup, dropping the Cortina name with its car connotations and renaming the vehicle the Ford One-Tonner.

It was in the half-tonne market that I was able to make a first contribution. The market development was favourable and pointed to the likely success of a vehicle derived from the Escort platform.

We had the fun of having all of the competitors in our product planning fleet and getting to drive them on weekends. They were all originally derived from car designs and some of the adaptations were crude with no engineering integrity; I remember the front-wheel drive Fiat, when carrying a full load, was impossible to steer in a straight line because of the torque effect and lack of fore and aft balance. At that time the Datsun/Nissan 1200 was the top seller.

Original design investigations are required to have a code name and one of my planners suggested a name which I did not want to use. "Believe me", I told the planning committee, which included Derrick and the engineering guys," this name will stick and we don't want our vehicle to carry this name"

Nevertheless we did use that code name and it did stick. The name was Bantam.

I was right and wrong. I was right that the code name became the model name, but wrong that it was a bad name for the market. Today the Ford Bantam competes for top selling spot with the Opel Corsa and the name Bantam is cleverly used to give connotations of performance, toughness and spirit.

During the time I was in product planning the South African government introduced a plan which was to turn the truck world on its head. For economic and strategic reasons (in those days everything was for strategic reasons, the economic was a smoke screen.) diesel engines were to be manufactured in the country and all commercial vehicles would be required to use only these engines. Manufacturers of commercial vehicles and diesel engines were invited to apply for the right of manufacture.

We competed in the truck market with the European sourced D-Series and the Lousville bonneted truck from the US. We did reasonably well in the below 16-tonne categories (the D0910 was a sales leader in its weight class for many years), but never enjoyed success in the heavy truck categories; it was clear a bid to build our engine would get nowhere; we would have to engineer someone else's engine into our chassis.

We all suspected the Mercedes-Benz engine would have the inside track; it was the market leader and was being used in military applications, so we opted for use of the air-cooled Deutz engines in our vehicles, arguing that they were specialist engine builders and would prejudice no-one.

I also suggested a strategy to Derrick that I know he liked and carried forward, but which I never heard the outcome of; I suggested we do a joint venture with Mercedes-Benz to market vehicles through our two dealer networks in which we would provide them with small and medium cars and pickups and would cease producing large cars and trucks, and they would supply us with large cars and commercial vehicles.

I was Product Planning Manager for several years, the longest assignment of my short career. But I was never going to qualify for the top job in Product Development, that would always go to an engineer, and rightly so, and I had to eventually move back into sales and marketing. Derrick Morris was amazingly understanding of my position.

The opportunity came to take a lateral transfer to the position of Field Operations Manager, responsible for the regional and district offices engaged in the sale of our cars and trucks.

CHAPTER 25.

Sales Operations.

I was back in the environment I love.

I had spent nearly four years doing project work, with horizons measured in years. Now my horizons were measured in days, weeks and months. Now there were daily problems to solve; now there were monthly targets to meet.

And I had daily interaction with South Africans, many with similar values, some of them mates from the old days. Doing operational work in a known environment, that was my happy lot.

The position was Field Operations Manager, responsible for the sale of the company's cars and trucks through the dealer network. My structure was three regional offices situated in Johannesburg, Durban and Cape Town, and nine district offices, seven of them situated in the regional offices, one in Port Elizabeth and one in Windhoek.

I reported to Keith Butler-Wheelhouse and the Sales and Marketing Director was still George Simpson. The reporting relationship was to prove to be a problem later, as I was not on the executive committee of the division, because I did not report to the Director, yet I was in the second highest ranked position in the division.

My regional managers were all people I had worked with in the past, some even old buddies, as was Sean Bownes in Cape Town. Sean was another Rhodes graduate, and another very good rugby player, and we had last worked together in the salaried personnel department as grad trainees. Sean was later to become Sales and Marketing Director when the company moved to Pretoria, working for Spence Sterling with whom he unfortunately had an unsustainable relationship.

In Durban was Duncan van der Poel. Duncan was originally a finance guy who took a chance and switched to Sales and Marketing, where he and I had worked together in the advertising field. Also in Durban, working for Duncan as a district manager, was one of my best friends, Des Bramwell.

The regional manager in Johannesburg was Malcolm McClelland with whom I had last worked in marketing strategy. Malcolm was the least enamoured of the three at my appointment and allowed these feelings to become known to some of his staff and dealers; a pity because he was a competent person.

I quickly found an opportunity to get the group together so that we could talk about the way they were doing the work, the impediments they found, what suggestions they had. What I found was a group who were being constantly interfered with, and who were in fear of George who had continued with his habit of believing the dealer before he believed his own people. The region managers were not sure if their views were being taken into consideration in Port Elizabeth because they felt they were living in a vacuum in the region offices.

The latter problem was the easiest to fix, I had them bring their regional order consolidation down to Port Elizabeth personally every month, giving them the chance to sit in at the meetings at which the production plans were discussed, and giving them the chance to air plans and problems of mutual interest.

The problem of George interfering was not going to go away but could be minimised by having him know what we were trying to achieve, giving him the opportunity to comment on our direction, making sure the measurements of performance were understood and relevant and reporting performance objectively. And the hard part; when he was in the wrong being prepared to defend the case, or the person.

One of the strengths of Keith Butler-Wheelhouse's management style is that he gives you your head once he is sure you know the important outcomes and are working towards them. So I was able to manage and motivate in my own way; the monthly reconciliation and planning meeting with the region managers, quarterly meetings with the whole group, visiting dealers with the district managers, thereby giving me the opportunity to see the effectiveness of the DM and a chance to get to know them better.

I always made sure that I fed back to the region managers my impressions of these trips, and particularly any problems they needed to attend to with individual dealers. I was conscious that they could see my interventions as undermining their efforts so I took pains to prove otherwise. That worked well with Duncan and Sean, and we developed an excellent relationship, which extended to their people and to the dealers in their regions; in their case I knew the good news was being spread.

Not however with Malcolm and I knew he was still trying

to undermine my efforts in subtle ways; with his people and with some of his dealers. To be fair to him he had the toughest region, handling the largest dealers and the ones with the direct lines of communication with George. He was also responsible for half of the country's sales.

My solution was to split the northern region into two, Johannesburg and the south the one unit, Pretoria and the eastern, western and northern Transvaal, Swaziland and Botswana the other. Mike Pittendrigh was appointed region manager of the Pretoria region.

I tried to involve myself with the district managers when the opportunity presented itself as it did when I found out that the Port Elizabeth based DM, Larry Kreuter, was interested in photography and was a member of the Port Elizabeth Photographic Club. He took me along to a meeting and I was soon also subjecting my photographs to the scrutiny of the judges.

Another less charming incident was having dinner with Phil Palmer and his wife in Johannesburg. They had two English Bull Terriers which kept a close watch on me all evening, the female sitting next to me at the dinner table and growling every time I moved too quickly. It was a slow meal!

We also had the chance in our quarterly meetings to socialise with one another and understand one another better. These meetings usually coincided with other events as was the case of a meeting we held at the Hilton hotel on the hills above Pietermaritzburg. From there we bussed to the Civic Centre in Amanzimtoti where dealer sales managers were being introduced to a new Cortina 5-link rear suspension designed by Derrick Morris; the introduction included a drive with Sarel van der Merwe.

The boys were always up for a party and I allowed myself to be persuaded to have the bus stop at various pubs on the way back and to continue the merriment in the superb Hilton pub.

On another occasion we went to the Riverside Hotel on the Vaal River for training on the upcoming Escort model. I was not satisfied with the dealer salesman training being done at the time and resolved to have the DM's do such training. So part of our meeting on the Vaal was that each DM would have to do a presentation on some aspect of the new car, which was to be videoed. And were they nervous; I caught Des Bramwell having a shot at mid-morning to calm his nerves.

The one evening the hotel arranged for us to have a braai alongside the river and we had a great time socialising together. I always like to challenge the younger set and my challenge was for them to organise Don Pedros late into the evening. I should have realised that they would go to any lengths and they did. The next morning I apologised to the hotel manager who took it all in good spirit.

We were all convinced the key to improving sales results was better training and operating procedures for our dealer sales managers. I undertook to develop a Professional Sales Manager programme with standards and procedures and a reward programme of the highest order.

We consulted widely with dealers to determine the best practises on a wide variety of subjects; prospecting, advertising, commissions, daily sales meetings, stock control, display, demonstrations and many more. The programme was introduced to dealers and was well received, and the DM's began monitoring progress, and finally they did audits to determine the best in the country.

I knew we would have different standards of interpretation throughout the country so I decided I would personally visit the top two or three dealers in each district to confirm the ratings. Bill Bayford, who had returned to Ford by that time and was working as George's Adminstration Manager, volunteered to join me. Bill and I had a great time visiting all those dealers and meeting such a wide range of interesting operators, all of them with their own ways of making money for their dealerships.

I was to take the Top Ten on the incentive trip and had the chance to plan it myself. We flew to New York for a two-day stopover, then to Detroit to visit items of interest and to do a training course, on to New Orleans for another course, to Orlando to visit Disneyland and finally a two night stopover in London. It was an outstanding trip, not least of all because of the personalities, some outrageous and profane, some conservative and sober.

In New Orleans, as part of the sales management course we were doing, we were asked to complete a personality assessment. I looked at my results and could not believe the stranger they described. This was not me, this was the person I had evolved into to protect the real me. I knew I had a big problem.

Chapter 26.

Disillusionment.

When did my belief in Ford Motor Company die? In answering my own question I realised that the process had been going on for a very long time and could recognise some of the headline moments, others were a subtle severing of small arteries to the spirit.

The first retrenchment we had at Ford was a travesty of justice. A decision was taken in Detroit to rid the company of 10% of its workforce throughout the world, irrespective of the performance of the various business units. In South Africa things were booming and we needed to grow, not shrink. But we had to take the knock nevertheless.

We sat at our desks, frozen, dreading the call to go upstairs to the board room where the unfortunate ones were being told they were no longer needed. They came back down to their desks, gathered their personal items and walked out of the building into the arms of the press.

Nothing kills your belief in a company to provide you with a career and an income for life for you and your family than an arbitrary act of retrenchment. A retrenchment properly motivated, with attempts at rescue seen by the staff, can be a different thing; if you can see for yourself what behaviour and performance results in you avoiding the chop, that can be different; but not by much.

The subtle signs were about frustration when good work was not rewarded, or could not even be appreciated because those reviewing it were not qualified. It was about the controllers becoming the dominant business force. It was about passion becoming routine.

When I first went to the US I found a winning company with winning people having a ball doing their jobs. On the last visit with the sales manager's programme I found a sad company with discontented people talking ill of the company.

My own reporting relationship was a source of irritation for me, decisions were being made which affected my department by the executive committee, more than half of whom were my juniors in terms of job ranking (that makes me sound like a corporate whiner, but imagine the position for yourself).

Sometimes you can claw your way back from these positions, many companies do. But there is one thing for sure; you can never perform at your best unless you believe in what you are doing.

It was time for me to move on.

PART TWO.

Mercedes-Benz

Chapter 1.

How not to change jobs.

I'll never forget how useless I felt in the three weeks between leaving Ford and taking up my new position with Mercedes-Benz.

It was my fault. I had done the unpardonable thing and burnt my bridges. And now I had to go to a new organization, where I knew only my boss, with no way back if I failed. I knew enough by then to know that failure was not just about your own performance.

Let me back up.

Dave Marshall approached me to join UCDD, the Mercedes-Benz distributors. I knew Dave from his days at Ford. He started as a grad trainee in the parts department and he was widely believed to be the director John Dill's successor in that department. That was when it was a separate division before being incorporated into sales and marketing.

After incorporation Dave spent time in various sales and marketing management positions at a senior level, before being given the assignment of Sales and Marketing director in the Philippines. I had always liked him although I wondered if his private school accent and cigar smoking habits were not a front. (Wrongly I found out, that was just him).

Dave had been head-hunted for UCDD where their Chairman, Morris Shenker, was reaching the age where he was considering retirement and wanted to spend his last years grooming a successor. Morris had really wanted Noel Philips but after he was appointed chairman of Volkswagen North America there was no chance, and he spread his net further. The plan was for Dave to be appointed Board Member for marketing and later chairman.

He found an almost total lack of systems and processes at UCDD and didn't really know how to fix it, not having spent time in the vehicle marketing trenches. On top of that the company was just a year and a half away from launching Honda which would bring new challenges.

The deal was for me to establish a marketing department and to be his successor when he took the top job.

Sometimes the difference between aspiration and reality is truly frightening.

Then I found out that he was also talking to Willie van Wyk about the same position. We phoned him on a party line and said that he was not playing the game, and should continue negotiations with one of us. I never found out if he did not have one last crack at Willie before continuing with me, or if Willie quit the scene because he felt Dave had behaved in bad faith in talking to the two of us. The truth was I was needier at the time.

Back to burning my bridges.

When I resigned I was called to Fred Ferreirra's office where he did his best to make me feel I had a good future with the company and they did not want to lose me. Then he asked me what they could do to keep me. I said if the Managing Director, Brian Pitt were to go I would be happy to stay.

I cringe when I read these words. It shows you how unbalanced a person can be when they are unhappy in a job; I guess it also shows you the corollary, how people can move mountains when contented in a job.

I was offered a position as a distribution clerk to serve out my time, or to leave immediately.

So I ended up sitting at home worrying. There were two incidents I remember from that time, one good and one bad.

Errol Richardson phoned me from Durban and said he heard I was unoccupied for a while and knew that was a bad feeling from his own experience; could he fly down and take me to lunch?

Now Errol and I had been competitors and had tip-toed around each other for quite a few years. For him in particular to make that offer gave me a tremendous boost. I will never forget his kindness and his words of consolation.

The bad incident came from Ernst Stockl, the Board Member for Finance and Personnel. Ernst later became a good friend, supporter and colleague. He phoned me, introduced himself and said he believed Dave had made me a job offer but he knew nothing about it, could I fly up to Pretoria and meet with him.

Dave had done his usual thing, gone out on a limb and not bothered with the detail. If the board member responsible for personnel did not know about my appointment what kind of job did I have and what about the promises for the future? I don't think I needed to take an aircraft, the butterflies inside could have carried me.

Ernst has a charming, affable manner which disguises a very keen brain. He had a piece of paper from Marshall who was overseas at the time which said make arrangements to hire this guy Cleary in the marketing department at R8000 a month.

Ernst was being very formal. "Do you know, Mr. Cleary that R8000 a month would make you a very senior person in our company". I was horrified; "Mr Stockl I am moving for the same salary as I was earning at Ford, and it makes me very nervous to hear that your salary levels are that low".

We then discussed the job I would be doing and he informed me about the benefits at the company. There was no mention of the second car I had been promised by Dave (in the position I had been in at Ford I could lease three cars). "What about the second car Mr. Stockl?" It turned out that they did not have a second car policy, not even for board members; it had been raised at a board meeting but not finalised (it took 6 more months to come into being).

I went back to Port Elizabeth, where I had no job, wondering what kind of boss I had and what I had let myself in for. I was not the happiest man on the planet.

UCDD never offered to pay for that flight and I never asked.

CHAPTER 2.

UCDD. (United Car and Diesel Distributors.)

There was a car displayed in the foyer of UCDD's offices in Schoeman Street on the west side of Pretoria. It was a chocolate-brown Mercedes-Benz 500SL with cream leather upholstery.

The foyer was as tasteful as the car with somber grays, black and chrome upholstery and concealed lighting. In fact the whole building was surprisingly good looking when you consider it had been an old-style motor dealership. It would always be a hodge podge and would get worse as the whole block was eventually bought to contain the growing company, but there was always continuity in style.

UCDD was in three main locations in South Africa; Pretoria, Durban and East London.

East London was the location of the assembly plants and originally started as a contract assembler (named CDA) for a number of car makes after World War Two. The original buildings were disused wool stores which came on the market in the periodic slumps in wool prices. The assembly plants must have been a nightmare to organize as they were widely spread on the West Bank; only in the 90's were all the in-between buildings bought, the roads de-proclaimed and the property consolidated.

Durban was the location of the parts store. It started as a joint venture of the original distributors in South Africa who named it MB Spares. Durban was the logical location as most of the parts came by ship and Durban was the closest port to the country's main markets in the Transvaal.

Pretoria was chosen as the location for marketing and administration at a time that import permits were required and it made sense to be close to government. It remained a good location as 60% of all motor vehicles sold in the country operate within a 150 kilometre radius of Pretoria.

Two floors above the foyer were the offices of Morris Shenker, the Chairman of the company. These offices, which included a board room and dining room, were particularly tastefully decorated and furnished. This was quite a difference from the utilitarian style of Ford Motor Company.

The Board portfolios of Marketing, Finance, Local Procurement and Product Engineering were located in Pretoria. Marketing was headed by Dave Marshall, who also had responsibility for parts, and Finance by Ernst Stockl. The head of Local Procurement was an interesting Hollander named Hein Te Poel who came to South Africa as a young man by driving through Africa in his DKW.

The final Board Member in Pretoria was Jurgen Schrempp, about whom so much has been written that it is hard to remember him in the context of 1981. Jurgen had come to South Africa as a young service engineer hardly speaking any English at that time.

In East London the production portfolio was held by a South African, Leo Borman who had been a management consultant previously, hardly an ideal background but he seemed to pull it off. He was a well known, even dominating figure in the East London community. The rest of the East London organization, the infrastructure and specially quality, was managed by Gunter Kamuf and he also managed the engine plant.

Stockl, Schrempp and Kamuf were Daimler Benz employees, giving the German company, even though it did not hold a majority of shares, control over the key functions of engineering, quality and finance.

I can write easily about this organization today, but it was difficult to comprehend when I started with the company and there was no help coming from organization charts. It was almost as if no one wanted to draw boundaries as that would restrict the opportunity to gain a little here, or lose a little there.

If you wanted to characterize this kind of organization you would call it organisation by patronage. If you were liked, or did a good job (sometimes not the same thing) you were given additional work. If you were a nuisance you went to work elsewhere. Leo Borman seemed to be the best at this game.

CHAPTER 3.

A new culture.

Within hours of starting work at UCDD someone mentioned to me that I should change before I saw Mr. Shenker as he did not allow the wearing of short sleeved shirts. I took his advice quickly.

It was an indicator that this was a very different environment.

And it certainly was. It was not only the German influence, the company had also attracted many Afrikaans speakers, specially in finance and administration, and a surprising number of what I would call academics, people whose main interest seemed to be accumulating second and third degrees. The inclination coming out of the background of most of the employees was to be formal and conservative.

I was in a state of extreme tension in those first weeks, still in the gloom of the three weeks of inactivity and the disconcerting interview with Ernst Stockl.

It was fortunate that I had previously had the experience of feeling alienated at Ford when working in different locations and countries with people of different backgrounds because what I found in UCDD was not my kind of place, things were too hidden.

I was to learn that much of this lack of openness came from the management style of Morris Shenker who dealt with the people he trusted, no matter their position in the company, to the extent that often the managers did not know what was going on.

Dave and I had a first meeting to decide what work I would be doing, and who would be on my staff. The name was the first sticking point, my area of responsibility was clearly the traditional marketing functions, but his title was Management Board Member, Marketing and he felt the use of the title marketing would be resented by the other people reporting to him. We compromised with the title Marketing Planning, not a great description of my job.

I was to be responsible for sales and product planning, pricing, advertising and promotions and media relations.

It soon became apparent that this job was going to step on everyone's toes. The two sales departments, commercial vehicles headed by Adolf Moosbauer and passenger cars headed by Christoph Kopke were used to making decisions on order levels, pricing and model range.

Christoph was the more supportive of the two. He saw the need to have more structure in these planning functions and he even helped me find the right staff from among his own people. But I was to learn that he was not about to let too much structure hinder his activities.

The most aggrieved person was Henk Onderweegs who had been responsible for most of these functions and now had someone between him and the board member.

In time Henk came to see that what he had been doing and

what we started doing were very different things. I separated his job and had him handle advertising and promotions but he was never happy working for me, and I was not enamoured with the way he handled the agency so eventually I played the game and let him go to Dealer Development to work for his friend Tertius DuPlessis.

I found we were doing some weird things. One of the people working for Onderweegs spent four or five days a month filling in a manual ledger of the dealer's used car transactions for Morris Shenker. I could appreciate a chairman who realised the importance of used car trading as an indicator of dealer health, but there were reports which provided this information, although in different format. Mr Shenker accepted my suggestion to use the report which didn't lose me five man days a month.

That first day of work, as I sat outside Marshall's office a tall athletic young woman had breezed in and brought light to the place. This was Delene McFarlane who was to be the first of many excellent people I eventually had working with me. Delene built a media and public relations office that was highly efficient and much appreciated by motor journalists.

As I started changing things, and introducing new processes, and bringing in new people, order came to my working life. I was more settled with my fellow managers, and they more accepting of me, and the outcomes of our work became more evident.

But there was a brooding problem that we all suffered, Dave Marshall could not settle disputes between his managers and this often meant lack of resolution which frustrated us all.

It was my good fortune to work with Dave in other capacities. We served together on the DaimlerChrysler dealer council as an example. When I left DaimlerChrysler, he, like Errol Richardson when I left Ford, was the only person to take me out to thank me. Dave is a decent man of the highest integrity with a great love for his family and Cathy and I enjoy the company of him and his wife Mary.

So I don't criticise Dave lightly. Unfortunately his lack of intervention caused divisiveness and it was clear that he no longer had the support of Morris Shenker who more frequently by-passed him.

He was not going to be the next chairman of the company. And where did that leave me?

CHAPTER 4.

Advertising Mercedes-Benz.

I had to find out what customer's thought of the brands in the luxury market.

I had some idea from research and experience with Ford Granada and Fairlane. But they were strictly small parts players. We had done a product acceptance clinic for Granada which included a test sample of customers who viewed the then unknown car with a Mercedes-Benz star mounted on the top of the grill. Perception of the car increased tremendously; estimates of the car's price went up over 20%.

And I had my own perceptions. Due to the fiasco over the second car, I bought a 7-year old Mercedes-Benz 220D. The quality of the paintwork, interior fittings and upholstery was better than the standard of many new cars of that time. And I could not help noticing the admiring glances of pedestrians; the car was that slow!

What fascinated me about the buyer experience research I commissioned was that the demographics of Mercedes-Benz and BMW buyers were almost identical. The perception in the company was that BMW were the aspirant group, younger and less wealthy. Not so. The age, sex and income levels of the two buyer groups were within 2-3% of one another.

But the BMW group rated Mercedes-Benz cars higher than their own car on every measure except performance. I had the survey respondents phoned to find out why. The question was; "if you rate Mercedes-Benz higher than your BMW on these measures, why did you buy the BMW?"

The answer: "One day when I'm older I'll buy a Mercedes-Benz".

It was a mental age thing. Very interesting.

Advertising for Mercedes-Benz when I joined the company was appalling in almost all respects; not enough money was being spent, the ads were lifeless, overseas material was being used almost irrespective of it's relevance, there was no television advertising, and no science or strategy in the choice of print media.

It wasn't the agencies fault.

D'Arcy handled the account and they had the best team of creative director and writer I ever worked with. Willie Sonnenberg and Terry Murphy handled the account themselves, even though they were in the top management of the agency. Later, even when Willie was Chairman of the agency he still handled the Mercedes-Benz account personally. Back then their motive was simple; they didn't want to expose other staff to the humiliating experience of writing ads for Mercedes-Benz.

In a later chapter I write about my admiration for Morris Shenker, but this was not his forte, nor did he have someone in the company to guide him.

Agency briefings were endless discussions of the features of the vehicle from overseas brochures. Morris insisted that the top people of the agency were present. The manager with responsibility for advertising in the company was not qualified and much more interested in keeping his job than facilitating good advertising through the agency. Communication with the agency was ad hoc and often destructive.

On one occasion the production people at the agency were so frustrated that they produced an ad with an offensive word hidden in the grass in the foreground of the visual. It was a measure of the trust we developed that they later showed this ad to me.

Not the environment to produce good advertising.

To his credit Morris allowed me to do the job once he trusted me. The process of earning his trust was stressful as I had to walk a tightrope in my defense of the really interesting advertising the agency started to produce once they knew that the good stuff would be run.

Most of the time I was with the company we produced ads which focused on the core values of the Mercedes-Benz brand; safety, comfort and reliability. Other ads focused on strengths of particular interest to South Africans and resale value was one of these subjects. Other campaigns were defensive, countering claims of the competition, and road holding was one of these.

The agency started winning awards. It was quite interesting to see their changing attitude to awards. Early in my friendship with Willie he told me awards were not an indicator of good advertising. That changed, specially when he saw how much more business he recruited on the strength of trophies proudly displayed in the foyer of their offices.

When you have a strong brand like Mercedes-Benz it is easier to produce great advertising. Only a brand with this kind of strength can use understatement, for instance.

Many of the ideas came from Terry Murphy. He was an avid reader of motoring matters and particularly anything related to the three-pointed star. He kept a scrapbook of this information, and media comments, and they found their way into the copy and even the concepts.

A case in point was an early ad which gained world-wide success. Terry read an article about the test track at Unterturkheim, Stuttgart. It described how the bank at the end of the track went almost vertical, pinning the car to the corner to the extent that it could steer itself.

Off they went to Stuttgart to get the picture. There were two problems, one of security, the other that only Mercedes-Benz test drivers could drive cars on the bend above 160 kilometres per hour because of the risk of blackout. Both problems were cleared and they got their pic. of a 280E model high on the bank with the driver holding his hands clear of the steering wheel. The headline read "You're holding this page tighter than he is holding the steering wheel". The ad was judged the best magazine ad in the world at the New York advertising festival.

The most important advertising awards in South Africa are the Loeries, which were a conservative affair in the beginning but which became an immodest celebration of the ego. I've no idea what they are like now, I stopped going long ago. But I am also being a little hypocritical because I am the proud owner of the Loerie which the agency won for Mercedes-Benz for the best advertising campaign (mixture of print, radio and TV advertising) in South Africa in 1985. They gave it to me when I left the company, and they could not have given me anything more valuable.

A campaign I remember well, for the opposition to it, and for its success, was the advertising we did for resale value.

The opposition came from the dealers who did not want us to raise customer's trade-in expectations. With the hindsight of now being a dealer myself I have more understanding of their point of view.

At the time, however, I saw only the opportunities. It was already a strength but I was convinced that awareness of the subject would put us a distance ahead of the opposition. The dealer might have to pay more for the trade-in but he could sell it for more. Sales of new and used cars should improve. We were also in a downturn in the economy and rational reasons to buy would get more attention.

As it turned out resale value has become a feature owned by Mercedes-Benz. The advertising we did at the time improved the resale values of our cars. Even today, when the advantage has almost disappeared, there is still the perception that Mercedes-Benz is the best in the industry.

I remember two of the approaches; a print ad with the headline "The buyer of this car has an advantage, one day he will be a seller", and a TV commercial with a simple visual of cars under black covers and a voice-over which went along the following lines "only eight cars bought in 1985 are still worth more than 75% of their original price, and all eight are Mercedes-Benz models (As the cars are revealed)".

The best ad the agency produced, perhaps even the best ad ever produced in South Africa, was the television commercial about a Mercedes-Benz going over the cliff at Chapman's Peak.

Terry Murphy read a small piece in the Cape Town newspaper about a driver called Chris White who survived an accident in which his car fell over 100 metres from the Chapman's Peak road. The car was a model W123 Mercedes-Benz.

This was not going to be an easy commercial. Apart from the technical problems with re-enacting the crash, Mercedes-Benz had a policy to never show a crashed car in promotional material.

The commercial required us to buy three W123 models, strip the engines and fuel tanks, equip them with remote steering devices, strap into them heavily protected cameras, roll them down the road and steer them over the cliff. Cameras were also positioned on adjacent sites, and in a helicopter. When you've only got a few seconds you have to give yourself plenty of opportunities to get the shot.

That wasn't the end of it. The Cape mountains have a very unique plant system which is rightly protected. We had to get permission to possibly damage it, although the area where Chris took the plunge consisted mostly of rocks. Finally we had to convince the authorities that we would remove the wrecks immediately, and have cranes standing by.

Chris White was very, very lucky. The first two cars fell on a trajectory that completely destroyed them. He would not have survived. The third car was badly damaged but would probably have sufficiently protected an occupant.

We overcame Stuttgart's likely concerns by not showing the exterior of the car. There are scenes of the car on the first part of the fall, and then the chaos captured by the cameras inside the car. The shock value is increased considerably by the horrific audio recorded from inside the car. At the end there is the sound of the door opening and a view back up the mountain, taken from the perspective of the survivor.

It was a sensational commercial because it was simple, dramatic and believable, and we received requests from Mercedes-Benz companies from around the world for the material so that they could run it in their countries.

The commercial gave the image of safety for Mercedes-Benz cars a tremendous boost. It was not just the ads, it received wide media coverage. And then, just when we thought it had run its course, BMW foolishly produced a copy-cat ad, and reminded everyone what great safety is designed into a Mercedes-Benz.

Improving an advertising idea of a competitor in a subtle way, not noticed by the bulk of the buyers, is not a bad thing to do. Producing a blatant crib is just plain tacky. BMW ran an ad with the concept that their car's superior road holding would have prevented the accident.

There were some other advertisers who copied the concept and we were absolutely delighted.

One last story amongst many.

The agency presented a story-board about a commercial they wished to make to promote the introduction of airbags in our cars (an old story you will say). A man was to walk off a building and fall onto an inflated bag far below. I assumed he would fall a storey or two, get caught in a net, and then by sleight of hand, fall again another storey or two into the huge bag on the ground.

That wasn't the way with Willie and Terry; they found a stuntman in Europe who fell 18 floors. Of course, he waited until there was little wind, but what a feat. I have a fear of heights and that helicopter shot of the man striding over the edge of the building still causes internal damage.

Chapter 5.

First success.

My first opportunity to show what I could do, and add real value to the organization, was introducing a new corporate identity programme in South Africa. The conference I organized to tell the dealers about the programme contained five addresses, and I wrote four of them.

In retrospect it is ironical that this was my first success at UCDD because I have come to regard the fickle changing of corporate identity as one of the worst aspects of the motor industry. Mercedes-Benz changed the corporate identity of their dealers three times between 1981 and 2006, almost once a decade. Each change was at enormous expense to the dealer.

That first programme brought me into contact with Heinz Bausch for the first time. I was introduced by Morris Shenker who told me, on another occasion, that they could burn Stuttgart, as long as they saved Bausch! He was responsible for advertising (including corporate identity) in Stuttgart, and that responsibility included a watching brief over the whole world.

The basic styling philosophy behind the change of the early 80's was to create an almost sterile environment in which the car became the focal point. Showroom interior colours were hues of grey with furnishings to match; outside elements used silver banding as an identity element. Signage on facias and pylons was in blue and white.

We were the first in the world to introduce these new designs, and the motivation was the imminent introduction of Honda in our organization. The Germans wanted to protect the Mercedes-Benz identity, the South Africans were happy to go along with it because it created maximum impact for the organization, and therefore for Honda.

But being first meant plenty of contact with the graphic designers in Germany, and plenty of changes, not only to the design itself but also to materials, as we had to find solutions from South African suppliers. Fortunately we had the assistance of an outstanding (in all aspects including cost!) design company in South Africa who earned the respect of their counterparts in Europe.

I also got to work closely with John Laubscher, and to get a better understanding of this very complex, morose man. John was an associate of Shenker's and had been hired as a consultant to assist with the Honda introduction. This was to include the implementation phase of the corporate identity programme, the toughest part.

Laubscher became the hammer, forcing time and action commitments from dealers. It was a role which was bound to cause great conflict, but a role he seemed happy to fulfill and I began to see why Shenker had hired him. I was glad that

I wasn't the one having to tell dealers to tear down the oak paneling in their offices! John seemed to do it with relish.

John and I spent a few days in Cape Town together visiting the corporate headquarters of the petrol companies, trying in vain to get them to accept elements of our identity on the forecourts of those of our dealer premises which they owned. To my surprise he let me do all the talking, perhaps he did not want to be associated with a failed venture.

Back to the conference.

I wrote speeches for Shenker, Marshall, Bausch and myself. Schrempp declined my offer.

Mine contained the biggest gaffe. I told the dealers that they would be able to pay for the programme from the profit of five cars. Not only was this an underestimate but it contained an arrogance which was lost on me at the time; it was as if dealer profit could be manipulated at the whim of the manufacturer.

Sadly, this is the case.

Chapter 6.

Introducing Honda to South Africa.

My first sighting of the Honda model we were to introduce was a great disappointment.

It was parked in the workshop at the back of the UCDD offices in Pretoria. A little, boxy, old fashioned looking car in the midst of the big shining Mercedes-Benz's. It's being a bit fanciful but it looked rather sad in that company.

Who would have believed that this little car was to become such a firm favourite among South Africans, achieving almost a cult following for its quality and reliability.

Lots of things had to happen before we achieved that status and I was supposed to deliver a whole bunch of those things.

Certain decisions had already been made about the car and they turned out to be excellent. The model was a Ballade, a derivative of the Civic, available with only a 1300 cc engine. But, most unusual at the time, in fact the Ballade established these trends among small cars; it was to be also available with automatic and air conditioner options.

As with the style there was great scepticism about these features. How would a 1,3l car with automatic transmission and an air conditioner perform at the high altitudes of the Transvaal?

The thinking behind it was very sound; the first customers for the car were bound to be Mercedes-Benz owners where these features were almost mandatory. They would expect to get them on the cars they would buy for their wives and children. It turned out that not only Mercedes-Benz second car buyers liked the features.

The car was definitely going to benefit from being built in the same assembly plant as Mercedes-Benz, in perception as well as reality. Many of the processes were the same; it used the same KTL dip process and paint shop, for example. It was not going to be possible for us to have dedicated paint lines for the Honda so it used the same paints as the Mercedes-Benz models, and they were of an exceptional quality.

Not that Honda gave away much on the quality stakes. The car had to qualify for the local content rules of the time and Honda were very particular about which parts could be made locally. They would not let us touch the engine, even though we made some of the parts, and assembled Mercedes-Benz engines. The Germans and Gunter Kamuf in particular, were miffed.

Honda was then, and still is today, the largest maker of engines in the world. They were very careful to protect their design and reputation in this regard. When engine designers in Stuttgart tore down a Honda engine they could not believe how fine the tolerances were. When we entered a car in the Total Economy Run in South Africa, they only gave approval after making the decision to build a special engine for us to install in the car.

We agreed a protocol with Stuttgart on the communication about Honda. We were not to publicise the synergies in the assembly plant, the use of common materials and processes. I had no problem with any of this, I believe when Chrysler started using parts, even whole systems, from Mercedes-Benz cars, it was damaging to the image of the latter.

We didn't need to draw attention to these matters, the media did. And the obvious connection could be seen at our dealers where all but the largest dealers had shared showrooms.

Not that we didn't use the fine reputation of Honda for quality, which was probably seen to have origins in the common assembly. An excellent TV commercial the agency made some time later showed a white glove lovingly stroking the fender of a shiny black Ballade to the music and lyrics of the song "Slow Hand". We were not about to tell anyone that cars built faster usually had better quality levels!

To nobody's surprise the Honda Ballade became known as the "small Mercedes".

My department had to plan and execute the advertising, launch, promotional material and literature. The positioning for the car was all-important and that clearly was to be quality, building on the fine reputation and sales successes of the brand throughout the world. A secondary objective was the unusual offering of air conditioning and automatic in this class of car with reassurances that the car could handle these systems.

We needed an initial print ad that delivered this positioning, and we weren't getting it.

John Laubscher had persuaded Shenker to appoint another advertising agency to handle the Honda account. Part of the motivation was to appease the rank and file in

Stuttgart. It was not something I would have done. I always believed one agency could handle different brands and the additional business made the agency strive even more and use their best people.

The agency appointed could not get the ad right, and it became an issue of principle between the creative director and me. Launch ads in print have to be informative. Consumers are most interested in products when they are new. They want to know everything about the product; doubly so when it is a brand never before seen in automotive guise in South Africa. We had a wonderful opportunity to get great readership about Honda in general and the Ballade in particular.

The agency wanted to produce a creative miracle.

Dave Marshall and I sat in Morris Shenker's office discussing the latest failed attempt. It was only a few months from the launch. Shenker was asking the questions;

"What are we going to do Peter.'

"I think we have to fire this agency and give the business to D'Arcy'.

"How do you do that".

"I'll make an appointment with their MD today and go to his offices to tell him we are taking the account away because they cannot produce the ads we want. We should offer to pay for the time they have spent".

"Can you do that".

"Yes, of course".

To Dave Marshall's credit he offered to accompany me. The meeting was most unpleasant as the MD of the agency, a Scandinavian national, chose to beg rather than tell us to get out of his office. He offered to give the account to another creative team and give us new results within days. Dave was looking too sympathetic for my liking so I declined his offer and we left.

I drove across town and gave the account to D'Arcy and briefed them. They had a mountain to climb in a very short time. They showed us an ad a few days later and we approved it.

A very big part of the successful introduction of Honda to South Africa was the training done by Christoph Kopke's people.

At the time of the Honda launch selling Mercedes-Benz was not a tough job; the car was in a dominant position at the top end of the luxury market, and in fairly short supply. Christoph knew that Mercedes-Benz salesmen were not going to get excited about Honda; he had to get dealers to bring in fresh young people.

The answer was the Sales Cadet programme, one of the most successful sales management development programmes I encountered (Until the Merseta system destroyed it by insisting on an irrelevant curriculum to earn credits for other qualifications and a financial subsidy). Years later those original cadets, who went through a military-style course lasting weeks, were amongst the very best sales managers and dealer principals in the organization.

Morris Shenker chose the Baxter Theatre in Cape Town as the launch venue. It was a decision in keeping with his personal preferences; he loved Cape Town and he was a benefactor of the arts. The Baxter played the more classy productions.

The launch was a mixture of information and glitz, with a Japanese theme in the costumes of a dance the promotions company produced and in the food we served. I had seen a magical gate in the sea off a sacred island near Hiroshima and

I wanted a replica of it to span the broad steps leading into the theatre. Nobody knew what the heck I was talking about and there was no Google in those days.

I eventually got my splendid Torii gate and the launch was a successful celebration of things Japanese.

CHAPTER 7.

First visit to Stuttgart.

I was in the office of the most powerful sales executive in the Mercedes-Benz world drinking schnapps at 9.00 in the morning.

Earlier one of his assistants had come into the office and announced they had received an order for more than 2000 trucks for delivery to Iraq. I got the impression that a lesser sale would have also have been toasted!

It was the office of the Management Board Member for Sales worldwide and I was on my first trip to Stuttgart, a trip that had been much delayed because Dave wanted to introduce me himself that first time. I did not mind the delays because I really appreciated his presence for the first visit.

That night he entertained us to his favourite Swabian restaurant, insisted I sit next to him, ordered my meal and ate off my plate.

I couldn't help comparing this behaviour to the way the Americans might have behaved. I was not thinking about the eccentricity. I would never have sat in the office of the top man in sales in Detroit, he certainly would not have entertained me and he most likely would have had difficulty pointing out where South Africa lay on a world map.

The Germans love Africa, mostly I suppose, because of their colonization of German East Africa and South West Africa. We had no problem getting senior Daimler Benz executives to come out for a visit and they often took the opportunity to combine it with a holiday, and many purchased property in Cape Town or the bushveld.

Our shareholders board always contained a few who were main board members, even past chairmen of the Daimler Benz board. All of this meant that they had a better understanding of our business which placed the company in an excellent position for those really big decisions, like building cars in East London for supply to the rest of the world.

I was to find out later that Honda also had strong attachment to South Africa, for strategic not historical reasons. They had decided to protect supply of platinum for their catalytic converters by buying a mine near Rustenburg. Every year the president of Honda came to South Africa to inspect his mine, and the mineworkers were given new Honda T shirts and stood in military lines to welcome him.

I love the feel of Stuttgart; the way the vineyards march down the hills in the centre of the city; the many forests in the middle of suburbia; the stout hostesses greeting you in warm, intimate restaurants where you could be in a private home. In my later years I was in Stuttgart five or six times a year, and I never tired of it

That first visit I was on the tourist route, the plant and design centre at Sindelfingen, and the museum, engine plant and test track at Unterturkheim. I met too many people to remember.

Two experiences stand out, the one a strange one you could say is no big deal. It was a hidden section where they make the laminated wood inserts for the instrument panels and door trim panels of the S-Class cars; the big deal to me were the many layers required to conserve the appearance of the wood but mostly to ensure that the wood did not splinter in the event of an accident. One of the many little things done for safety.

The other was the high speed laps around the test track. I do not like being out of control in a car piloted by someone else at speeds at which a car should really crash. The test driver who took me around had very little English, but I remember him saying to me "look, look", then he jerked the car violently to the left and right and left again and then let go of the steering wheel! The car centred itself and he said "see, is a good car".

Of course, it was a Mercedes-Benz.

CHAPTER 8.

Morris Shenker.

Morris Shenker possessed the most important characteristic required of a brand builder; consistency.

He passionately defended the Mercedes-Benz brand and kept it on track in all his years of stewardship over it.

His first major defense of the brand was before my time but he spoke of it often. During one of the fuel crisis periods it became anti-social to own large luxury cars. Customers, specially senior figures in industry and commerce, parked their Mercedes-Benz cars in the garage and commuted in conspicuously small cars.

Morris went on the attack conscripting the two Murrays, Stuart and Hugh, both respected financial journalists, to his cause. A survey was developed for publication in the Financial Mail, the most influential magazine of its kind, and an important source of information for our clientele.

The survey argued that a Mercedes-Benz was a sensible and economic purchase. It had excellent fuel consumption and very low repair costs. And its resale value was the best in the industry; in those days of high vehicle inflation the car could often be sold at a similar or even better price than the original price.

The article, and others like it, gave customers the arguments to get back into the cars they loved.

The first major issue I was involved with was when Car magazine gave the S Class car a pasting for poor fuel consumption.

One of the things we could absolutely rely on in those years was the fuel consumption statistics given to us by Stuttgart, and published in our brochures. Something certainly was amiss because the Car magazine figures were considerably worse.

For Morris it raised the specter of the times when Mercedes-Benz was regarded as an opulent extravagance. A whole bunch of us were called to the boardroom and Morris vented. He called Norton Ramsey, publisher of the magazine and a personal friend of his and expressed his disbelief in the results and questioned the qualification of the writers. He ordered Jurgen Schrempp to take an engineering team to Cape Town to inspect their equipment and observe their road test procedures.

It turned out that their equipment was not performing to spec. Jurgen had a picture of their fifth wheel off the ground during operation.

Norton was conciliatory and the magazine bought brand new equipment recommended by Mercedes-Benz. They retested the S Class and reported a much improved result. The magazine saved face by making the retest part of a story on the new equipment and the better data they could now give their readers.

The incident had another unintended outcome. At the

time Norton's son Alan had recently taken over the reins as editor of the magazine and he was angry at his father interfering in the integrity of his editorial team. Delene McFarlane and I were doing our best at damage control because Car magazine is the single most influential medium for the motor industry.

We must have got through because Alan and I became close associates and had a warm relationship whilst I was at UCDD. When I left the company to become a dealer he phoned me and said he had told his subscription people to give me a free copy for life.

Morris preferred to maintain a formal relationship with the staff. Only with the inner circle was he more open. He could be cynical at times and most were wary of him.

So I was not at ease when I heard that we were to be sitting together on an aircraft from Hamburg to Tokyo via Anchorage. But I was glad I did because he opened up regarding many subjects that I had wanted to ask him about. On that trip he invited me to call him Morris, a privilege I only used in private or in the company of others who also had a more relaxed relationship with him. He was, after all, older than my father.

I was to learn on the many trips we took to Tokyo together, and on other social occasions, that he was charming, and knowledgeable on a wide range of subjects.

Sadly Morris Shenker died without enjoying time in retirement.

CHAPTER 9.

The South African office at Daimler Benz.

I was having a ball, driving a Mercedes-Benz 190E 2.3 16-valve, as fast as I dared on the back roads down to the Bodensee. In the car was Manfred Altmann, from the South Africa office in Unterturkheim, and his wife and son. The road was clear and we were on a trip to see the Lake of Constance.

Lunch was in an exquisite restaurant with views of the lake. I still remember the name, Gashaus Fischerhaus because it was one of the best meals I have ever had. Or maybe it was the surroundings.

They had asked me to bring a costume in case we wanted to swim and we stopped in a lay by next to the road. The lake was a short distance away. "Where are the change rooms?" I asked. "We change here on the side of the road", said Manfred.

Not a chance, I stumbled 100 metres into the forest. On the rocky beach there were women bathing topless, something I'd never seen before. Manfred's son was obviously aggrieved at something and he was in the water waist deep when he took off his shorts and threw them to his parents on the shore. It turned out the Altmann family owned a cottage on the nudist island of Stilt in the North Sea.

By the time we returned to the car my inhibitions were considerably reduced and I changed in full view of the road. The cultural influence of Europe!

Heinz Bausch had arranged for me to go into the holiest of all holies, the design studio at the Kuppelbau, a large circular hall with amazing lighting; it threw no shadows. I had a chance to talk to one of the designers and asked them about their approval process, interested to compare to the Americans; did they use consumer input? No, he said, how could a customer know how a car should look so many years in advance.

In those days the product lifecycle of a Mercedes-Benz car was eight years, and the design had to be approved two years before production. Imagine trying to design a car which had to remain fresh for ten years? He explained that they helped to orientate the board when it made the decision by first showing them a really radical design, predicting taste twenty years out, then they showed them the car they wanted to be approved.

It certainly fitted with my logic; the taste of the consumer is determined by what is already on the market. Creativity belonged to the designers.

The South African office in the sales division at Daimler Benz merited a full office staffed by four people because of our importance as an assembly operation and pretty good volumes; we were the fifth largest market for the S Class model, after Germany, the United States, Japan and the United Kingdom.

The office was headed by Fred Quest who had two excellent qualifications for a manager in the "head office", a doctorate and silver hair. I jest. Fred was not at ease with my more informal manner but he did his best to understand and help me. Certainly he and his wife were thoughtful hosts and we had two memorable Sunday outings, one to the mediaeval town of Rotenberg, and the other to a French village in the Alsace region.

There was something else Fred was not at ease with, the decision to market Honda in South Africa. It turned out that the rank and file had no understanding for the decision. I was seen as the one who had brought about this state of affairs. I became known as "Mr. Honda" and constantly questioned on the rationale for the move and what I was seeing in Tokyo, and being asked to compare organizations. It was an awkward situation.

It turned out that Morris Shenker took his strategy right to the top, the Chairman of the main board. He by passed Fred Quest and many others who greatly resented the slight to their person. I was a welcome target. My opinion is that Shenker would not have got to first base if he'd tried the regular route.

Fred didn't turn down the invitation to the Honda launch in Cape Town!

CHAPTER 10.

Safety.

Contrary to popular belief among American consumers Volvo did not build the safest cars, Mercedes-Benz did.

I use the past tense because today judgment on this issue has become a matter of numbers. The European NCAP safety standards have become the universal measure. According to this measure the safest car in the world today is Renault.

But does NCAP tell you the whole story? I worry, for example, at the weighting given to the buzzer to remind you to fasten your seatbelt.

I was constantly surprised at the depth of concern to produce the greatest safety measures in Sindelfingen (where safety research is conducted). It was not about finding an advantage to market Mercedes-Benz, it was about saving lives. Most of the designs, although patented, were released for use by other motor manufacturers.

From the 1950's Mercedes-Benz started buying crashed cars in the Baden-Wurttemberg area for intense study. I do not know if this programme is continuing but it was certainly providing much of the information which was the source for passive design introduced during my time at Mercedes-Benz of South Africa.

The statistics revealed much that was not commonly known. Two pieces of information I remember well, one of which was to have a huge effect on car design.

The less dramatic finding was the high prevalence of ankle, foot and lower leg damage to the driver. This was because in most accidents the driver has his foot jammed at full strength on the brake at the same time that the brake pedal is pushed into the car by the force of the impact. Brake pedal design was changed so that a cantilever effect took the brake pedal away from the driver.

The studies revealed that the highest prevalence of all accidents was the off-set frontal smash. Understandable, when you think about it; it would always be your inclination to avoid hitting something.

It was not common knowledge.

In the US cars were required to pass crash tests for homologation. These tests included a full frontal barrier test. I remember when the 5 mph bumper legislation came out and caught all the manufacturers by surprise, so that they had no time to properly design for this requirement and bumpers that year stuck out to a ridiculous extent. That legislation required the car to withstand a full frontal impact at 5 mph. without the bumper intruding into the body of the car.

I am giving attention to the situation in the US because this is the single biggest car market in the world by a distance. All manufacturers want to market their cars in the US and therefore they all had to design their cars to meet these standards. For some manufacturers these were the main standards they designed to meet.

When you design a car to pass a full frontal barrier test the longitudinal section of the middle of the car must be strong. Ironically this is not the best design if the car is going to be hit on one of the corners.

I've seen pictures of some of the cars Mercedes-Benz crash tested at their facility in Sindelfingen. In one car, from a well-known luxury car competitor, the pedals penetrated the stomach of the dummy in an offset smash at only 60 kph. Most American designed cars did not fare well; many of them had engine and gear box intrusions into the passenger cell.

Don't be concerned! Mercedes-Benz released these research findings to the automotive world and today the offset smash forms part of European and American homologation programmes.

If you are lucky you might never get to experience the life-saving qualities of safety designs.

Take the seatbelt pre-tensioner as an example. My wife and I were in an accident with a vehicle without this design. The location of the accident was remote and we only saw the damage to our bodies caused by the seatbelt some days later. The seatbelts probably saved our lives, but seatbelt pre-tensioners would have reduced the severe bruising and muscle damage we sustained.

I was a dealer by the time the fantastic active driving systems began to be introduced into cars. My only knowledge of them comes from two incidents driving Mercedes-Benz cars where we would not have avoided the accident without them.

I believe no motor manufacturer spends as much time and money building safe cars as Mercedes-Benz.

One needs to not just look at the feature list because the quality and effectiveness of the feature should also be taken into consideration. When we launched the 190E cars to the motoring press in South Africa we were entering a class of the market where Mercedes-Benz had not competed previously and I did some research into the competitors in this class.

I found a different level of design for airbags. I was able to say "Don't think because two cars both have two airbags, or four, or whatever number, that they are equal. In the class in which the 190E competes the Mercedes-Benz has airbags which have 50% more volume and inflate twice as fast as competitor cars".

One last story illustrates the attention to detail. In a board meeting Hein te Poel informed us that they had made the decision to locally make the steel seat base for the S Class model. "I hope you haven't changed the design", I said.

"Why?"

"Because the front of the base has a raised section to stop the occupants submarining under the instrument panel".

Chapter 11.

Launching new models.

Nowadays cars sneak on to the South African market. The problem is model proliferation. There are just so many models for each brand that even the industry watchers have trouble knowing them all. What about the average consumer?

The problem is made worse by the increasing use (chasing the Germans) of alpha-numeric nomenclature instead of a proper name.

Motor manufacturers and distributors do little more than a press release for most of the models they launch, with perhaps a media launch if it is one of the volume sellers of that brand. Launching to the dealer is a dying art; if it is done it is usually to coincide with a dealer meeting of a general nature.

All of this puts more of an onus on the dealer to provide the differentiation for the customer at the point of sale, which in turn means the salesperson becomes the one to position the model for the customer. Even with salesperson training on the model, and insistence on brand focus for salespeople, this is a hit and miss method of marketing a product that cost multi-millions to develop.

Positioning, which is the art of placing a product in a cubby hole in the mind of the customer, becomes something for the brand, and not for the individual model. So, if the brand positioning is large safe cars, as Mercedes-Benz used to be, how does that new sporty small model fit in?

Confusing, isn't it?

The amount you spend on the launch phase of a product life cycle also depends if you believe in impact or reach.

Well I'm an impact man and I think much more could be done to properly launch and position each new model, so that it has a chance to penetrate its own market niche and not just cannibalise other models in the brand.

Let me tell you about some of the more successful car launches we did.

We decided to launch the third Honda Ballade model in East London. The first model had been launched at the Baxter Theatre in Cape Town, and the second at the Wild Coast Sun. East London was where we built the car, alongside Mercedes-Benz, and we wanted dealers and the media to see this connection.

The problem with East London was the lack of a venue. There seemed to be nothing that could hold an audience of around 150 people for a show and reveal, followed by a sit-down dinner.

Then someone suggested the city hall, which was an attractive building from the outside. Inside we found two halls, one a beautiful, but dilapidated, room with an arched roof, the other a very old-fashioned hall with a stage and a balcony on three sides.

We lit the beautiful room to hide the age and used it for the dinner after the show. The hall we changed much more radically; the audience sat on the balconies (after the engineers assured us they could hold the weight), and we hid the lower floor by stretching a new floor across it. The car came through the floor for the reveal.

The city of East London gained from the event because we covered the chairs on the balconies with leather we could not use for our Mercedes-Benz cars because of some flaw not visible to the average eye.

When we eventually launched the C-Class car in South Africa, we did it with a bang. The promotional company handling the job came up with a concept of a musical, in which the fate of a theatre was dependant on something new, the something new being the C-Class car when it was revealed.

The audience sat on the stage, which then moved backwards revealing the sets which were lowered to the position the audience had occupied just moments before. With some haunting songs and some of the best singers in the country, it was an enjoyable and memorable evening for dealers, the media and a few hundred customers.

To my embarrassment Heinz Bausch, who had been invited to attend the first night, was so overcome with emotion that he hugged me for longer than your average man can take! But I recognized the compliment; Heinz got to see launches of new cars throughout the world and he had never seen anything quite like ours.

A major launch for us was the model W124, because it coincided with the 100 year celebration of Daimler Benz. We created a walk-through museum of the models down the years, each placed in a setting depicting the times, including mannequins dressed in clothes of the period.

It was a big hit with the traditionalists, who make up a large proportion of Mercedes-Benz customers, as can be seen by the following of the Mercedes-Benz Car Club.

I was delighted and amused by an incident which occurred when we launched our first 1,6l Honda model to the press in Cape Town. I invited my son to join us. He was studying at Cape Town University for a Business Science degree, majoring in marketing.

The event started at a wine farm with a dry lunch and presentation of the car, and then we moved to the Killarney race track. Part of the programme we had prepared was a sprint down the main straight from a standing start, culminating in a reading by gatsometer of the speed attained. There was to be a prize for the fastest driver.

My son came to me and said, "Dad, these guys don't know how to accelerate with front-wheel drive cars, they can't keep the front wheels on the road" I thought it was typical youthful bravado; he was talking about the best motoring journalists in the country.

That evening we transported everyone by open double-decker bus to Hout Bay and had dinner together. At the end of the evening I stood to say thanks and announce the awards from the driving experience. One of my people handed me the list of winners. At the top of the list, fastest down the straight, was Andrew Cleary.

There are some modern examples of doing it the right way; the best I experienced was Guy Franken's re-introduction of the Dodge brand to South Africa, and the launch of the first model, the Caliber.

Dodge positioning is bold, brash, American. They hired

Gold Reef City for the week and turned it into a cowboy town. Television commercials and print ads confirmed the positioning with risqué approaches that brought freshness to car advertising. Dodge Nitro material has built on the theme.

It must have been very expensive, but the results have been excellent; Caliber continues to sell higher volumes than expected, Nitro quickly became a cult car.

So what is expensive? Expensive is the car you don't launch properly that soon becomes another unknown name among the many hundreds competing for that cubby hole in the buyer's mind.

CHAPTER 12.

Jurgen Schrempp.

Before Jurgen Schrempp became Chairman of the South African company he did a stint in the US, running the earth moving equipment company Euclid which Daimler Benz had bought. It seems his main job was to sell it, which he did.

When he arrived back to take up his new post in South Africa, the accounts people strung a large banner across the entrance to the building in Schoeman Street in Pretoria which read, "This business is not for sale".

Schrempp took up the vacant management board position of marketing which he was to hold until Morris Shenker retired. Not too long after that Morris became ill and retired earlier than intended.

It was decision time for who was to become the new management board member for marketing and Schrempp chose a different course; he split the portfolio into passenger cars and commercial vehicles with me taking the car job and Adolf Moosbauer the commercial vehicles job.

Unknown to Adolf and me, Jurgen had been lobbying this split in Stuttgart because it was not a common arrangement at that time.

While I was to benefit from the splitting of the function along product lines I believe it is the right thing to do.

I had seen a similar organization at Ford where the tractor operation was separate and worked extremely well. The issue is the question of whether customer groups behave in a manner which is sufficiently different to warrant separate focus.

Commercial vehicle customers do require different approaches; much of the buying power is in the hands of large transport companies, and there is a technical and service orientation arising out of the high cost of fuel and maintenance in the operation of a commercial vehicle. Commercial vehicle customers were buying an expensive commodity.

Of course the split functions had shared services; the dealer network was common in most instances although there were a few dealers which handled the products out of separate facilities, and parts warehousing and distribution was common to both.

In our case the parts function was transferred to Rainer Jahn, Schrempp's successor in his old engineering and service job. The blending of the two after market departments is a common choice, as long as neither parts nor service dominates as they have fundamentally different business philosophies. Dealer development, which dealt with dealer establishment matters, became my responsibility.

So, at age 40, three years after joining the company, I got the job I desired.

I wasn't kidding myself about the luck of it. If Christoph

Kopke had not been forced to leave the company he would have been Schrempp's first choice, almost irrespective of the relative experience and ability of the two of us.

Kopke and Schrempp and their families were very close in the years when Jurgen had just arrived in the country and welcomed the company of another young German-speaking family.

Then Christoph got fired because he had used his entrepreneurial spirit to buy a car wash machine on one of his trips to Germany and had not informed the company; there could have been a conflict of interest. Unfortunately Christoph's second-in-charge, Fritz von Olst also had to go.

It was fun and exciting working for Jurgen Schrempp.

I remember the social times more than I remember the business decisions we made. He is a charismatic and passionate man who leads the group rather than the individual. Despite his humble background he had the self-confidence to mix with, and even dominate, groups of important business and government leaders.

And, because of his humble background he was much loved by fleet owners, the security establishment and his old staff from service. Some of the parties with transport company owners and his police buddies, which were held in the chairman's suite, became legend.

He is also an expansionist. We bought a company plane to carry the Pretoria-based board members to a weekly board meeting in East London, and to be used for senior managers to visit customers and dealers. Used properly it could be a marvelous promotional tool.

The trips back from East London became champagne fests; often the first bottles were opened before the plane, a KingAir, left the runway. But the talk was always of business, usually going over the decisions of the day and the mood was usually celebratory.

The longest party I recall was at the time of the launch of a new Honda model in East London. It was to be a strenuous week with launches on separate days to dealers and their staff, to the press, to customers and to our own East London staff.

We stayed in the old King's Hotel, since demolished, to have some privacy from the other attendees who were in the main hotels. Schrempp found a piano in the disused ballroom in the basement of the hotel and with Jahn on the piano, and plenty of sustenance the party was on!

We would repair to the rocks on the seashore for his tradition of a cleansing ale and retire to bed before the sun came up. This went on for five nights in a row, and attendance was compulsory.

Ernst Stockl was to be rotated back to Germany and his successor, Sepp von Hullen came out to understudy him. His first board meeting was a disaster, with him immediately trying to show his knowledge on every subject and trying to force his opinion on our decision making. After the meeting Ernst took him aside to tell him to moderate his behaviour; unfortunately only with partial success.

So I was flabbergasted and distressed to hear from Schrempp that Von Hullen had been appointed as his successor months later. "You can't be serious Jurgen, why didn't you stop it? You know it will be a disaster" was my reaction to the news. Schrempp claimed that he had no choice; the decision was forced upon him by the main board in Stuttgart.

I still wonder if he really tried. He was to be appointed to a new job as head of commercial vehicle sales worldwide which he could only take up once a successor was installed.

As shocked as I was, my first thought was how my managers would take the news. Von Hullen's arrogant and petulant manner had become common knowledge and Schrempp had been a popular chairman. I needed to put a positive spin on it.

In the meeting with my managers I told them that it had been a good time with Schrempp but the company needed to consolidate and Von Hullen was probably the man for this job. I asked for their support for this next phase in the company's development.

I never knew who it was, but one of them told Schrempp about the meeting and the discussion. I also never knew if I had been fairly represented in the re-telling.

Schrempp told me I had been disloyal to him and that was the end of our business and personal friendship.

Sepp von Hullen was not a good leader. Two stories illustrate this, one rather petty.

Sepp and I were together to attend the reveal of a new Honda model at their R&D center north of Tokyo. In the middle of our price negotiation he told me I needed a haircut. I told him to cool it, this was an important discussion and he was making our hosts nervous. He persisted.

On the way back to South Africa I stopped over in Hong Kong, my favourite city, and stayed at The Peninsula hotel. In their hair salon I had a $150 haircut which I later charged to the company, hoping he would hear of it and challenge me, but he never did.

Von Hullen did not like to meet with dealers. I think he was afraid of being challenged by persons he did not have sufficient control over. Theo Swart, who was then running McCarthy Motors, asked me to arrange a meeting with Von Hullen to be attended by him and Brian McCarthy.

On the Sunday night Sepp phoned me to say he couldn't make the meeting. I asked him why and he said he was too busy. I tried my hardest to persuade him, stressing that Brian McCarthy was probably the most respected dealer in the country, his Mercedes-Benz dealerships sold nearly 20% of our cars and trucks, and that I knew he had flown up from Durban to be available for the early Monday morning meeting. He became defensive and repeated that he was too busy.

I phoned Theo and tendered my apologies on behalf of my company and offered to meet with them in their Pretoria offices. That meeting was extremely awkward and I learnt the depth of their frustration at being unable to meet with our chairman to discuss matters critical to the future of their Mercedes-Benz business.

Eventually that incident and many others emboldened the dealers to take the unprecedented step of going to Stuttgart and asking for Von Hullen to be removed. They were successful.

Back to Jurgen Schrempp.

There was a sequel to this story which played out in Tokyo. I was the guest of Rainer Jahn who had been appointed President of Mercedes-Benz Japan. Jurgen was in town for meetings with Japanese manufacturers and the three of us went out to dinner together.

The subject of my disloyalty came up and dominated the conversation. I had my first opportunity to defend myself, and even attacked him, saying he was the disloyal one in allowing Von Hullen to get the job in South Africa. Rainer strongly supported me but we got nowhere.

When we got back to the hotel Jurgen suggested we go for the traditional cleansing ale and we found a small karaoke bar in a side street. Jurgen started singing German songs in his strong deep voice, much to the dislike of the small group of men at the bar. One in particular, a fit–looking man in his mid-thirties was particularly aggrieved and becoming increasingly aggressive. I smoothed the waters and we shook hands. He had callouses like a sixth finger on the underside of his hand.

I believe I saved Jurgen Schrempp from a severe beating that night.

Schrempp was a king maker. If you stayed loyal to him he would take you along with him. Loyalty was the most important value and some appointments were made on the strength of this quality alone.

What else was his legacy?

The splitting of the marketing portfolio was one (unfortunately Daimler has since reverted to one marketing head). But his biggest legacy was born out of his love for South Africa. Although he is a German patriot, South Africa is his adopted country and he has given generously of his time to serve on government advisory boards.

He has done much to put South Africa on the world map and I'm sure he took the lead in the decision to build Mercedes-Benz cars in East London for export. Today if you go to dinner in Tokyo in a C-Class car it will be one made in South Africa.

CHAPTER 13.

Hong Kong.

Hong Kong is an assault on the senses, and was for many years my favourite place of retreat. Strange as it may seem I could always connect with my inner being in a place so different, so filled with turmoil of man and sea.

In the last chapter I described a visit to Japan. As it turned out I travelled often to Japan to do business with first Mazda when I was with Ford, and then Honda and later Mitsubishi during my Mercedes-Benz years. I usually travelled alone and always made a stay-over in Hong Kong.

I developed a routine for my Hong Kong visits. The first action was a walk to the ferry station and a ride across the busy harbour on the Star Ferry. Only then could I indulge in my other favourites; a walk around the peak; Peking Duck at the Jade Garden on Nathan Street (I once took a group of motoring journalists there with the promise of the best Peking Duck in the world; I received no dissent!); a ferry ride to Cheung Chau island.

Let me describe the Cheung Chau experience. You take

the ferry from Victoria Island. It is about a half hour journey on a large ferry which comes cautiously through the hurricane moat into a harbour filled with junks and sampans. Along the harbour quay is an odd mixture of buildings; restaurants, outboard motor repair shops, fishing equipment stores and private homes. At one end is a Buddhist temple, seemingly out of place with its quiet and dark interior and smell of incense.

Cheung Chau has no motorised transport but that is no problem as it is easily traversed on foot in less than an hour; a walk through old China. On the harbour wall there are dozens of tin trays with fish kept alive by water pumped into the trays from the harbour. You choose and purchase your fish and take it to a restaurant across the street where they turn it into an exquisite meal.

For me the magic of Hong Kong was not only the sights and smells, it was the stimulus it gave to introspection. Somehow a place with a ridiculous level of overcrowding, with heat and constant rain in summer, and that busy sea, could allow me to retreat into my thoughts.

This poem describes it best;

Victoria Peak.

I am in Hong Kong again
surviving the twists and turns
of the flight through the buildings
emerging into the bedlam of noise and traffic.

This is a city
of exquisite beauty and decadence
where the vastness of the human experience
allows you to be truly at peace with yourself.

On the peak
high above the heaving dark-green sea
an old man
reads the writing on my hand.

His ancient yellow eyes
fix on the converging lines
and see not just the present conflict
but the unfolding
of a much more rewarding time.

As I descend back to the crowded streets
I realise how glad I am
that I received this sliver of hope
in my favourite place of solitude
among a million indifferent souls.

CHAPTER 14.

Meridian.

For too many years our focus was inwards, but with the East London situation stabilizing, we could again look to the market and the work we were supposed to do.

We found many needs of our customers to address, particularly in the fields of insurance and financial schemes and products. We tackled insurance first.

In the late 80's and early 90's, before hijacking became a major problem in the country, Mercedes-Benz cars had an enviable reputation for being difficult to steal. We knew from police records that the percent of Mercedes-Benz cars stolen was around half of the percent of Mercedes-Benz cars in the population. We also surmised that the accident rate of Mercedes-Benz cars was lower than the norm because of the profile of customers.

But the insurance companies did not give customers credit for these things in terms of lower premiums. We intervened on behalf of our customers by calling a meeting of the major insurance companies to which we also invited the police, and which was also attended by engineers from Stuttgart. We demonstrated the superior locking systems of our cars, and the police showed their records.

The insurance companies did not budge. They obviously relied on the good claims record of their Mercedes-Benz clients to offset losses elsewhere.

I asked one of our managers, Peter Azzie, to find us a solution. He found a young broker named Rob Thompson, who worked for a broker accredited to Lloyd's of London, and who he believed could offer an insurance product for Mercedes-Benz and Honda customers. Rob's youth and appearance (he wore a pony tail in those days) hardly pointed to success in this venture and we had fun putting him in front of the dealer council.

But Rob did deliver; he developed an insurance company that gave a superior level of service for exceptional rates. His claim procedure was the best in the industry. He also developed some unique benefits, for example your car could be replaced with a new car in its first year (no depreciation) and he would supply alternative transport if the replacement car was delayed.

Rob's insurance offering was the first in a series of services that we developed for customers.

The next major area we tackled was finance.

The floor plan arrangements for our dealers were done through Nedfin, a division of Nedbank and they should logically have been our partners in developing financial solutions for our customers. Unfortunately it didn't work out that way and it might have had something to do with an earlier disagreement.

When I had taken over sales a few years earlier I found that my area managers were doing floor plan audits for

Nedfin. This was a conflict of interest; I could not have my people whose primary job was to promote dealer sales also performing a policing function. And it could have led to a dispute in the event of losses. I put a stop to it which obviously resulted in Nedfin having to incur additional costs to perform this function.

I took an idea to Ron Rundle the Managing Director of Nedfin. We were experiencing a slow down in sales of our S Class cars due to an economic downturn and this was a scheme which would allow stepped payments by customers as they could afford more.

Despite a few reminders I heard nothing from Nedfin so I took the idea to Stannic who put the scheme into practice within weeks.

That particular scheme was not successful but as is the case in so many of these schemes they bring customers into the showrooms and you eventually sell the car in a way which suits the customer better.

Ron complained to Ernst Stockl, claiming that the stepped finance scheme was their idea. Clearly he did not want to do business with me.

I really wanted a relationship with Wesbank the largest motor financing bank and I got a chance when I and some of my managers were invited to one of their Friday luncheons.

I prepared a document for their MD, Peter Thompson showing that although Toyota was the market leader in South Africa, the largest company in terms of monetary turnover was Mercedes-Benz. And after all, did they make their money out of the number of units they financed, or the volume of capital financed?

Our approach was followed up by Neville Nightingale, then the number two at the bank and later the MD. Neville started exploring opportunities with us and we ran a few schemes to test the mettle of our two organizations. We both liked the experience and it developed into a joint venture which was beneficial to both organizations. We got the benefit of their superb field organisation to understand and promote whatever scheme was running, and they had the inside track to finance our customers.

We were fortunate to have people who understood vehicle financing and risk. Peter Azzie was a maverick but he understood the business. Carlos Waelkens, who was then our company Treasurer, had an astute understanding of risk and markets. These two people played a big role when it came to financing with residual values. Carlos did a lot of work towards the contractual arrangements we made with Wesbank.

Wesbank were never greedy. They understood that if the schemes were not made available to all banks we would sell less cars. This is a principle not understood by the managers running the in-house financing for DaimlerChrysler products today; they apply enormous pressure on the dealer to give them the lion's share of the business with a negative result on sales, due to their high qualification criteria for customer approval.

There was a satisfying development to the joint venture with Wesbank; my wife and I became personal friends with Neville and Marita Nightingale, a relationship which endures today and we have the delight of sharing holidays and special celebrations together.

When I became a dealer and was losing money Neville decided to test the strength of our relationship be giving me some strong advice; "Do you want to be the biggest dealer in

Empangeni, Pete, or the richest?" There was much more, but that's the bit I remember.

As we developed an increasing number of customer benefits we needed a name to embrace them. We could not use our brand name because these benefits also extended to Honda. The search was on and the race was won by Japie Kuhn who suggested the name Meridian.

Meridian was Peter Azzie's baby and he attempted to add numerous new products and services to it. Our problem was to hold him back, and ensure that there was structure for each of the new products; cell phones, credit cards, holiday schemes, anything our customers desired could be obtained through Meridian. (A precursor to the value adds services being offered by the chain stores, banks and companies like Discovery today).

I need to be careful not to sound like I am defensive about the things which were developed under my watch, but I am a marketing man and I try I can see things from a customer's point of view. Daimler Chrysler lost a lot in ditching Meridian and what it had come to mean to customers and suppliers.

Today when you visit a DaimlerChrysler dealer you can have Mercedes-Benz Finance, Mercedes-Benz Insurance, Mitsubishi Finance, Mitsubishi Insurance, Chrysler Finance and Chrysler Insurance (I left out the Fuso and Freightliner options!)

The best aid to market focus is always simplicity.

CHAPTER 15.

Doing it my way.

During the years that Schrempp and Von Hullen ran the South African company I had the marketing job pretty much to myself.

Of course certain aspects of marketing, specially advertising and product design will always be in the public domain and you will find experts everywhere. But experience teaches you how to handle this interference, even from your boss. And one should always keep an open mind in areas of creativity and taste.

But by and large I could do it my way and I had the time to build properly.

It starts with organization and systems, and that requires an understanding of priorities.

During the Morris Shenker era we did an interesting exercise, facilitated by IBM, to determine the most important decisions to be made by the company, and at what level the decision should be made.

It had started with Morris calling me to his office to

complain about the increasing cost and application of computerization, and to ask my opinion about the proposal from IBM. He saw it as a sales gimmick from the computer giant to sell more hardware. I told him we were in the dark ages in terms of system development and application and the company could not grow unless we embraced computerization.

The IBM study found that very few decisions were ranked at the five-star level, the level most critical to the success or failure of the business. The five-star issues in marketing were planning volumes, product selection (not design because we had no design capability), branding/image and distribution strategy.

The marketing department had to choose the right product, plan the right volume for the product, build and maintain an image for the product, and provide the optimum distribution of the product to the market.

Choosing the right product and planning its volume is the work of marketing planning; building and maintaining the image is the work of advertising and promotions. The optimum distribution of the product is planned in dealer development and supported by sales, service and parts, which are instruments to help dealers realize their potential.

Marketing planning was always my first love, and it is where you should start your brightest young people. They must learn the discipline of sales planning, and the value of proper research (not only market research) to support decisions.

We were fortunate to have that department run by a succession of professional planners who had a mixture of discipline and mentoring in their management styles. The result was some bright young graduates who received their grounding there, and used the experience to springboard their careers. Three who come to mind are Le Roy Muntingh, Dianna du Preez and Liesl Eales.

The person who ran advertising and promotions for us, successfully and for many years was a secretive and distrustful and sometimes brilliant man. I came to hear about Japie Kuhn, who was then a regional manager under dealer development, because I was looking for someone to help the agency do their job, and I was told Japie did wedding photography on weekends.

Strange recommendation, I thought, but perhaps evidence that he possessed some flair. And he sure did. Once Japie learnt to give the agency their head they produced some of their best work. Similarly he developed good relationships with promotional and design companies and could be relied upon to produce launches and promotions of an exceptionally high standard of creativity and execution.

The home based functions of our dealer network management, dealer planning and sales distribution performed adequately, but we did not get the regional offices right until much later when service became part of my responsibility.

If you have a situation where you have three board members claiming authority over the dealers you need extraordinary co-operation between those three individuals to make it work. We certainly did not have that; we had a turf fight which was damaging to our staff and did not produce a culture of service towards the dealers.

My philosophy is simple. The department from whom the dealers derive their highest level of profit is the department they will give most respect and co-operation to, and therefore should be the department which takes the lead in the management of the regional office.

I inherited a system where the regional managers reported to dealer development as this was seen to be a neutral home for the person who had to co-ordinate sales, service and parts activities for the betterment of the dealers.

I changed their reporting line to sales, but that was unfortunately seen as a threat by my colleagues and they encouraged their people to maintain their independence. The dealers were the ones who suffered because they no longer had a partner in the region office to help them with their problems.

It was during these years that I evolved a management style that worked for me and resulted in a higher level of performance through improved morale and co-operation.

The key is communication and transparency. I insisted we had weekly meetings of the people reporting to me. There was no formal agenda. The weekly meetings required the managers to resolve differences and led to understanding and trust.

I also had the weekly meetings at the end of the day so that time was not a restraint, and a more congenial atmosphere could be created after hours. We always had a well stocked bar in my office. Sometimes the conversation continued for many hours, but it was almost always about business. Many fresh approaches came out of those sessions.

Understanding and trust, the important ingredients of team work, were further enhanced by strategy sessions we held in remote locations. Sometimes these sessions had a specific purpose, such as the annual budget submission, but more often they had a theme which could be a new marketing idea, or a way to improve our management performance.

An example of the latter was embracing the six thinking hats of de Bono as a means of improving decision making through a structure that allows divergent views to emerge.

If time and money would allow it, we involved partners. One of these was a budget session which we held at Thornybush in the eastern Transvaal.

We drove down on the Thursday and did most of our business in a number of meetings until late Thursday and through Friday. Our partners were flown in by the company plane on Friday afternoon and a more social programme followed for the rest of the weekend. Importantly, it included a session in which we explained our targets for the forthcoming year to give understanding to our partners for our work and priorities.

There was an interesting cameo to that weekend; when the aircraft turned around at the end of the airstrip its nose wheel came to rest against a raised concrete section. Keith Hawksworth, the pilot, had to gun the engines to free the plane causing a dust storm of epic proportions to rage through the lodge.

We tried team building exercises of a physical nature but they were unfair on the less fit ones in our management group. One noteworthy example was a three-day excursion into the Drakensberg foothills. The first part of it was a long strenuous walk over pretty tough terrain from where we left our cars. The intention was to discover the route through clues left in the equipment and on the trail.

We needed leadership and I was not going to provide it. The group became quarrelsome and some were struggling physically; Stan Bromley was near retirement age. Finally, Peter Azzie and Eric Scoble sat on a bridge over a mountain stream and refused to go any further. It got pretty ugly, and our guide had to reveal that our camp was on a plateau around 200 metres above that place.

I was at my happiest and most productive in those situations with my management group when we were developing new ideas about our business and how to manage it. But my ordered life was about to take a more chaotic path; it was announced that Christoph Kopke was to replace Sepp van Hullen as Chairman of the company.

Chapter 16.

Christoph Kopke.

"You needn't worry Peter; I fix things that are broken. That's what I'm good at. If I stay longer than five years I'll destroy the company".

These were the words spoken to me by Christoph in our first meeting. I had phoned to congratulate him, and we had met at his Waterkloof home.

I sometimes wondered if he had forgotten his own advice. But he left a big legacy, certainly much more than his predecessors. Some of the ideas he introduced were world firsts.

Christoph had his priorities worked out. It started with fix the organization, and then fix the labour problems in East London. To start fixing the organization he used a facilitator he had used previously at Lindsay Saker on his Porsche division. He kept assuring the board members that this would be a logical process and no-one could be aggrieved because it all made sense.

We met at Mpekwene, a beach resort south of East

London for several days and it was a logical process, but there were winners and losers and the aftermath was to continue for a long while.

I inherited passenger car service which allowed me to fix the region office problem. Erich Glanz ended up with an organization focusing on commercial vehicle engineering and service, a logical combination, but he was not happy; it was the beginning of his increasing dislike of Kopke.

Fixing the organization became much more than that first exercise with the board. Christoph was very taken with the Japanese ideas of conformity and equal worth. This was no better illustrated than by a visit to the Honda R&D center north of Tokyo. When you arrive you are required to take off your jacket and wear a white dust jacket, reducing all to equal status.

East London was a very unequal organization with structured and entrenched levels of management and favour. And equally entrenched racism.

Christoph attacked these ills with the fervour of a puritan; he has that in his make-up. Get rid of the status symbols and the many levels of management and you start to have people interacting without false barriers, at the same time align the functions to ensure accountability, what he called "Lines of Business".

There was a particularly famous meeting of all management from East London, Pretoria and Durban at a lodge on an outcrop of ancient granite hills near Brits. It was called Dikololo; the name became synonymous with loss of privilege. Grading structures were changed, organizations aligned, benefits reduced. It was also the first of a series of retrenchments which were to become known as the October Fest; ironical for a German company.

Essential to the fixing of the labour problem in East London was the realization that management was equally at fault. That was not an easy one to swallow. I was often told in Stuttgart, sometimes by German managers who had never visited South Africa, that the problem was the Xhosa people, they were argumentative and lazy. We would never solve the problem of strikes unless we moved the plant, preferably out of South Africa altogether.

That opinion came directly from the managers in East London, who had to account for a loss of production averaging thirty working days a year for five years and culminating in a nine-week strike and sit-in.

The first objective report came from a young labour lawyer, Louis Vermaak, which was tabled at a board meeting, held in East London. He talked of the gap between supervisors and labour, how it was artificially maintained, how the union structures were undermined, how supervision encouraged competition between the two labour unions to keep them weak and how some supervisors were so afraid they locked themselves in their offices.

Out of all of this arose the concept of a partnership with labour, very much driven by another young labour lawyer, Ian Russell, who was to become board member for personnel. The union was engaged and given standing; full time shop stewards were appointed and recognition given to their pivotal role. Some of the union leaders of that time rose to national rank in the movement; some became managers in the plant.

It's hard to believe that the East London plant has become a model of stability in the South African context, enjoying more years of industrial peace then any other motor plant in the country; that those same argumentative and lazy workers now produce cars for export to the world at standards of quality sometimes even better than some of the German plants.

But first there was a last ditch attempt at chaos, the nine week strike during which around 300 workers occupied the plant for weeks. Video footage of that intrusion still has the power to shock, workers dressed in white gowns made from material found in the plant, brandishing wooden models of machine guns, toyi-toying around mock coffins labeled with the names of the hated white bosses.

I had a small role to play at the end of the strike. Christoph and his family went on a much needed holiday overseas and he asked me to go to East London while he was away. In the two weeks I was there the most important thing was to establish a sustainable pattern when work resumed.

The work force was going to be short of the workers who sat-in at the plant and had been dismissed. I suggested that on the first day we have the remaining staff go to their work places, establish the shortages, re-assign the remaining staff, send them to their new work stations, ensure they knew what their assignment was and then send them home without doing any work.

It was a control mechanism, but it also said that the old order was not going to work; we had to tackle this thing with a new mindset. It was not easy to persuade the managers to adopt this strategy, particularly Hans-Jurgen Wiegand the board member for production, but eventually everyone came around and the strategy was a success; day two was a day of energy and enthusiasm.

Persuading the plant managers to accept my strategy on the plant reopening would never have happened had I not spent many hours cultivating a relationship with them. In the automotive manufacturing world there is a huge chasm between the plant and sales, with both sides critical of the other.

Luckily my experience in product planning and personnel in earlier years had given me an understanding of the values and mentality of plant people. On many occasions I took the time to stay over in East London to have dinner with manufacturing colleagues; on one occasion we played tennis and drank red wine at Gunther Kamuf's house until the early hours of the morning.

Through these many experiences Hans-Jurgen Wiegand, Ian Russell and I became more than just colleagues, we actively supported one another.

It took a person of courage and determination to work through that seemingly impossible situation in East London. And Christoph Kopke certainly has those qualities. He is afraid of nothing.

In all the difficulties we had more bad news; the whole board was summoned to Stuttgart to appear before the Daimler Benz main board. We all believed we were going to be fired; except perhaps Christoph. In a somber pre-meeting he was his belligerent self and he carried the bluff into the critical meeting with the main board.

I think we got away with it that day because he attacked instead of defending, and surprised them into a better opinion of the South African board.

CHAPTER 17.

New ways to distribute vehicles and parts.

In terms of the narrative timeline this chapter should occur later. The programmes it describes were in their infancy at the end of my time with DaimlerChrysler, and came to fruition when I was a dealer.

However they describe Christoph Kokpe's finest accomplishments and seem more in place here, after the chapter on him.

One of Kopke's driving forces was the elimination of waste, and none more so than the inefficiency of distribution systems. To help him on this mission he found a consultant called Warwick Johnson. Warwick was working with the parts people in Durban and did a presentation to Kopke who promptly hijacked him to his own cause. In all Warwick must have consulted to DaimlerChrysler for a decade.

He tackled the waste in the vehicle distribution systems first.

All motor manufacturers operated a system of selling vehicles to dealers who would, in turn, find customers for them. This is called a push system, the vehicle is pushed to the dealer and then pushed to the customer, and it has many inefficiencies. Chief among the inefficiencies is the duplication of stock in the manufacturer's stockyards and the dealer stockyards.

With computerisation there is the possibility to have only one stock listing, and to have the vehicle delivered to the first customer who wants that particular vehicle anywhere in the country. But to do this the manufacturer must own all the stock, no matter where it is stored.

This is called a pull system because the customer's choice drives it.

The other area of waste was the duplicated transport costs which came from the high percentage of vehicles the dealer would swap with another dealer to satisfy his customer.

Simply put then, DaimlerChrysler would own all the stock and only release the vehicle if there was a signed customer order. Dealers could not own stock, if a car they ordered for a customer was subject to a cancellation that vehicle would return to the manufacturer's stock for re-assignment.

But the dealers needed to have vehicles for display and demonstration and for this purpose a new demonstrator programme was introduced; vehicles would be supplied free of interest for 120 days; the vehicle could only be used for display for the first 45 days, and could only be sold from day 90.

It sounds simple but the NDP (new distribution system) needed major work in systems development, the questions of carrier performance and dealer training. Unfortunately it also resulted in the development of draconian fine systems to ensure the dealer complied.

It resulted in a totally different philosophy of selling for the dealer and their salespeople. Whereas a car could be delivered out of stock in one day previously, you now had to order the car from elsewhere in the country, usually taking around a week, or the car would come out of forward production with a waiting period of many months at times. The salesperson had to manage the customer during this waiting period.

The salesperson also had to be computer literate and disciplined and ended up doing far more administrative work and therefore had less time to sell.

The manufacturer also had to change their sales philosophy. If they wanted to move a particular model they would have to devise a promotional programme whereas previously they could merely incentivise the dealer and leave it up to them.

In my opinion these were the plusses and minuses.

Firstly it achieved what it was designed to do; you could sell many more vehicles out of any given stockholding. Dealer stockholding interest costs were eliminated. We were better able to satisfy the customer's individual needs; if the car was coming out of forward production you could sit the customer in front of a computer and have them specify the exact car they wanted. Costly and dangerous (the first car we had written off was a dealer swap) dealer swaps were eliminated.

On the negative side were less productive salespeople, the system was not as suitable for higher volume fleet vehicles where early delivery was essential, and demonstrator write-back costs were high on some of the models.

Overall though, NDP is an outstanding system for customer satisfaction, dealer profitability and efficiency.

Sadly I do not think the current young German managers at Mercedes-Benz of South Africa understand the value of the system. A push system would suit them better as their primary objective is to make a name for themselves whilst they are in South Africa.

The change to the parts system was an even more dramatic departure from traditional methods.

Once again the main culprit of inefficiency was a duplication of stockholding at the manufacturer and at every dealer. Again, computerisation could create a national stock file and the manufacturer would have to own all of the stock at every dealer point.

But this change would require a lot more planning, and a massive change to computer systems to achieve. The business concept was thrashed out between the parts people and dealers; dealers would be paid a selling commission for parts they sold from the store, and a stocking commission for parts they received at the store to hold on behalf of DaimlerChrysler. Parts transferred from one store to another earned another commission.

DaimlerChrysler wanted a uniform design of store, mainly for security and audit purposes, and set standards of performance which determined the stocking commission they paid; these included the time taken to bin a part on arrival, the time to pick and deliver the part and a perpetual stock take system. All of these standards were measured by the computer system, which timed every action.

Profit calculations were made to ensure that dealer profitability was not reduced, and these had to take into account the additional investment required by the dealer to revise, and expand their stores, and the benefit they received at not being required to own parts stock, a very large portion of a dealer's assets.

I know for us, when this change occurred at Inyanga Motors, the positive cash flow of selling our parts stock back to DaimlerChrysler was very welcome, although cynically we could say we soon needed to invest ten times the savings in new buildings which brought little value to our business.

DaimlerChrysler was able to divest themselves of their own huge store in Durban and place all stock at dealer points close to the customers. This meant a massive growth of stock at the dealers; at Inyanga Motors in Empangeni, our stock grew from R3 million to R12 million with obvious advantages to our customers. DaimlerChrysler now operates a docking station near Oliver Tambo airport in Johannesburg whose only function is to receive parts and re-assign them to a dealer point somewhere in the country.

A key part of this distribution system is the change of dealer computer systems. At the time the most used systems by dealers were Kerridge and Automate; both were given the opportunity to revise their systems to accommodate the requirements of DNI (Distributed National Inventory). Only Kerridge complied which was a great pity as we found it to be the weaker system in terms of accounting practices and CRM, and it required more people to operate it.

DNI and NDP changed the world for DaimlerChrysler dealers, giving us a competitive edge in efficiency and customer service with improved profitability. I cannot believe others have not followed; perhaps they need a CEO with the vision and conceit of a Christoph Kopke.

CHAPTER 18.

Cosmos.

In 1986 my wife Sandra and I separated and I went to live in Cosmos, a beautiful and remote hamlet which clings to the south slope of the Magieliesberg mountains on the shore of Hartebeestpoort Dam.

In retrospect I found that place out of an instinct to survive. I was the instigator of the separation and filled with doubt and self-pity. But I had a job to do and could not allow myself to perform below my best. Cosmos was the balm; my instinct had driven me to my roots, a remote place in the bushveld.

In a way my life became like the time I lived on my own in Detroit; I lived between an office in Pretoria and a townhouse 40 kilometres away in Cosmos. There was little else. On Sundays I would walk up the mountain behind the hamlet and over it to a four-way stop where there was a filling station and I could buy the Sunday newspaper. The return trip was via the tar road; in all the journey took around four hours out of the worst day of my week.

The complex I lived in was mostly for week-end occupation and only me and an old man who fished for barbel every night lived there during the week. In those days the zoo across the dam had lions and I would be woken early by their calls; it was the signal to go for a run and swim before leaving for work. Most nights I returned after dark, often as late as 10.00 p.m.

Over twenty years later I managed to put that experience into words. This is the poem I wrote about those times;

Cosmos.

The hoarse grunts of the zoo lions
Echo across the dark waters
Calling the new day.

As my feet pound the road downhill
Light enters the world
Creeping down the mountain
To land warm on my face.

The punishment of body
And beauty of the place
Expel the demons
Ready for one more uncertain day.

I am in purgatory
Living between two lives
No firm footing wherever I tread.

The attempted reconciliation
A journey through night in heavy rain
Tail lights of trucks dimly seen
Visibility made worse
By eyes misted with self-doubt.

Pounding the road downhill again
At the dawn of a new day.

Multitudes of seed birds
Rise ahead of me like blown leaves
In the bush the haunting call of the tschagra
On the flank of the mountain
The lazy rising spiral of vultures.

All around me this evidence
Of a wonderful design.

It's not about me.

Others will have their say
And I will drift into certainty.

The following year I moved back into the city to a townhouse in Irene and there Cathy and I got together. Shortly thereafter we moved to a small holding in Glen Austin which we developed into a beautiful home in which we spent eight years.

It was a measure of our distrust for the institution of marriage that we did not marry for six of those years. And then an incident occurred which changed all of that.

I had built a paddock and stable and we kept a Connemara pony which Cathy's daughter Caryn rode. The horse was playing up and Cathy, who had been an extremely able rider and show jumper in her teens, decided to teach it a lesson. Unfortunately her skills were a little rusty and she was thrown, landing on the small of her back.

Caryn's desperate cries drew me to the paddock where I found Cathy lying and unable to move; we both thought she had broken her back.

In that unromantic setting and strange circumstance, I asked her to marry me.

CHAPTER 19.

The war between Stuttgart and Munich.

Southern Germany has three of the finest makes of cars in the world, and two of them are engaged in mortal battle.

A few decades ago the battle lines were clear, BMW made small sporty cars and Mercedes-Benz made large safe cars. That was until they started invading each others' territory and the battle plan got messy.

BMW made their cars safer and spent more development money on their bigger cars and SUV's. Mercedes-Benz made smaller cars and more sporty models, getting involved with AMG and McClaren to give the strategy credibility; both examples of line extension gone too far.

They also both felt the need to grow beyond their main business, and BMW was much smarter in this regard.

In the 1980's I started to get this vibe on visits to Stuttgart. Nearly everyone was a strategy expert and the message was Mercedes-Benz could not survive on their car and truck business alone. The buying started; aeroplanes, marine engines, railroad systems, white goods and over one hundred computer software houses, amongst many others.

Disaster, nearly all of them have gone.

Growth strategy phase two was engineered by Jurgen Schrempp. The strategy was to become a major player in the automotive business world-wide by owning one of the motor companies in each of the three big markets, Europe, North America and Japan, and maintaining a close eye on Korea.

Chrysler was purchased, a major share of Mitsubishi was obtained and a minor share of Hyundai followed. At least it was in the motor industry and it should have had a chance. Shareholder pressure, the lack of results and probably apprehension about culture differences killed them off.

I often feel these grand strategic moves owe more to ego than rational plan. Man's desire to empire build often trips him up.

BMW got involved with Rover, ditched Land Rover after a short honeymoon and kept Mini which they have built into an interesting niche player.

I had ambivalent feelings about making smaller cars. I knew it would deteriorate the image, and it has. Mercedes-Benz is no longer exclusive, special and focused. But I also thought it was probably a better business plan to have a broader base. I had no ambivalence about maintaining standards. Stuttgart went through a period when they believed they had to launch one new major model every year and design the cars to a cost level dictated by the market. We did not need cars of the quality of the first models of the A-Class and the ML.

The South African market was for long a protected market because of the local content programme. We could only afford to build the forerunners of the E-Class, and the S-Class, and we assembled a few SEC's a month. The other models were imported in low volume because they were expensive due to the high import duties.

We had to decide whether to include the upcoming C-Class in our production programme. Schrempp was Chairman of the South African company and he wanted the car. He had the decency to allow me to make up my mind and suggested I visit Europe and investigate performance of the predecessor model, the 190E.

It's called manipulation but it beats autocracy hands down.

We made the decision in favour of the C-Class and were able to import 2000 units of the 190E to tease the market. They sold easily.

Who is winning the war between Mercedes-Benz and BMW? The one with the more consistent focused strategy of course.

Chapter 20.

Providing leadership for growth.

Not only was Meridian the fruit of our renewed assault on the market after the years of strikes, so too was a dramatic improvement in our market shares for both Mercedes-Benz and Honda.

By the mid-90's we had some of the highest market shares for both brands in the world, and certainly the highest market share for a single Honda model of any market, anywhere.

This came about because of a stable management team, a focused approach, and some   outstanding people.

I have already described a few of these managers in earlier chapters, Japie Kuhn and Peter Azzie. There were two other key players, Eric Scoble and Fritz von Olst and there could have been a third, Le Roy Muntingh; unfortunately in an earlier move I had to choose between him and Eric for a key position. I'm sure I could have kept Le Roy with us if I had handled it in another, better way. His later career showed the error of my choice.

Eric came to us from Toyota, where he had replaced Albert

McClean as market research manager. I interviewed Eric on the verandah of our home in Glen Austin, a story he loved to tell. He started in our marketing planning department and very soon made a name for himself with enthusiasm, innovative ideas and an excellent grasp of markets. He was soon to shed his nerd image, something I'm sure he does not acknowledge today!

I persuaded Fritz to rejoin the company after he had been with Porsche and doing other jobs for a few years. He started as Regional Manager in the Cape, one of the most sought after jobs in our organisation except for the constant need to provide transport, and sometimes entertainment, for the host of visiting German dignitaries.

After a while back in Pretoria Fritz became taken with the mood of the country and the ideals of our social revolution in East London. I encouraged him to follow his dream and admired him for doing so. He worked for some time in logistics in a German plant and ran a production unit in East London.

Fritz was back in harness and provided the disciplined approach and historical grounding for the team. There were others who did not hold the big sales and marketing jobs but provided variety and brought their own unique character to the mix. In the line of business concept of Christoph's I ended up with responsibility for aspects of finance and had the skills and experience of Koos Burger to count on, and I had responsibility for personnel in Pretoria, which brought Theo Swanepoel into the team.

To this group of people I brought my leadership style; inclusive, working with the group, setting higher targets and standards, demanding accountability, seeking social contact with the team and families and exploring new ideas.

Of course there was conflict and some of it was created by me because the socialising became a way of life for a few of us who enjoyed each other's company away from work, and particularly because our partners got on well together. This created some division because of my perceived favour for these managers.

But the division was more a question of style and background and had to be managed for the good of the organisation; each person was making a contribution and the group had to recognise that. The weekly meetings were invaluable; they brought conflict to the fore, the first step to solving it.

There was plenty of fun and unity also. I remember a frivolous discussion on how to dispose of the S Class hearses which Azzie had imported (you're right; about as bad a marketing idea as you can imagine!). Someone suggested the advertising line "If your life has been a mess, take your last ride in an S".

But mostly it was all business, setting the goals, writing and implementing the plans to achieve them, celebrating the success with the staff, re-planning the failures, discussing tactics.

Our planning meetings at remote locations delivered a wealth of ideas and some astute predictions of future movements in the industry; for example, years before it became a reality we predicted that the dealer groups would become major competitors, obtaining the distribution rights for brands not yet available in the market; today AMH almost competes with the market leaders in total vehicles sold.

A great idea which went nowhere was to increase sales of Honda by creating boutiques with merchandising orientated to women buyers in the larger Woolworths stores; that was before there were boutique showrooms in shopping centres.

I count my last few years at UCDD/Mercedes-Benz of South Africa/DaimlerChrysler South Africa as among the best in my working life, rivalling my year as a District Manager at Ford, and the time I ran Field Operations. The common factors were the people I worked with, and that very much includes the dealers, and the ability to create space to achieve.

Unfortunately my space was being invaded by a bored Christoph Kopke, seeking space for his ideas.

CHAPTER 21.

The right way to change jobs.

I always knew that I would have to move on when Christoph began meddling in my business. We were fortunate that the priorities of the company kept him occupied elsewhere for a much longer time than I had anticipated.

And when he did start to interfere, there was no objective reason to do so. Our growth record was outstanding, the best in the country at the time, image was improving, and dealers were satisfied. It was a happy and successful unit.

There had always been differences in our leadership style and our approach to marketing. People used to say to me that Christoph was a marketing man and I would smile inside; Christoph is a logistics man.

He always used to say he had no trust in advertising because half of it was waste. He never took the trouble to find out which half so he preferred to spend advertising funds on sport and community promotions, stylish promotions but at enormous cost per customer reached.

His puritan nature always led to him seeking to put the

cheapest version of a model on the market. We had quite an argument about the Colt double cab; he believed there would be a market for a low cost version with smaller engine, normal suspension and no features. Such vehicles had flopped before and so did ours.

Sometimes I was surprised at the degree of difference in our taste. Early in my time with the company, when Christoph and I were colleagues, he was urging Dave Marshall to sponsor the cricketer Clive Rice who was then and remains today a controversial figure; at the same time I was not allowing the agency to include people in our ads because they would typecast our cars.

Ironically I would have had no problem with the radical changes Christoph wanted to make to the distribution systems for vehicles.

When it was inevitable that conflict would become unmanageable unless I compromised to a degree that has never been possible for me I approached him and said it was time to move on. He was supportive in assisting me to look at options but there were very few because I was not interested in an assignment out of Africa.

Sadly he gave my management team a hard time after I left. He chose to run it himself as a committee, not providing leadership on a daily basis and letting the question of a successor drift. They did their best to keep the teamwork going, but the environment was hostile to such an approach.

PART THREE.

Inyanga Motors.

Chapter 1.

The wine bottles.

There are 10 wine bottles in my pub that have labels reflecting some of the key events of our innings in motor retail. They were given to me by my managers as a memento in 2004 when I turned 60, and updated in 2007. They make a good introduction to this section of the book. Here are the labels, in chronological order;

1995.	Inyanga Motors.	Third Street/ Lood Avenue.
1996	Inyanga Motors	Ngwelezane Road Bronze Street. Inyanga Plaza.
DAU Motor Holdings.		1999 Empangeni 2000 Richards Bay.
2000	Peter Cleary.	Zululand Chamber of Business. Businessman of the Year.

2002	Inyanga Motors	Chrysler/Jeep Sales Achievement Award. CCSI Award.
2003	Inyanga Motors.	DCS Dealer of the Year. PC Service Manager of the Year.
2004	Inyanga Motors	Chrysler/Jeep Dealer of the Year Vryheid.
2005	Inyanga Motors	Best Market Centre. 10-year anniversary. Empangeni. PC Service Manager of the Year.
2006	Inyanga Motors	Dealer of the Year. Vryheid Business of the Year.
2006	Inyanga Motors.	DaimlerChrysler Chairmans' Award.

Not a bad scorecard, but I can't help thinking how bland they are without the colours of history. The brush strokes would be black in the beginning, gradually lightening to the colours of joy.

Chapter 2.

Inyanga.

As we walked down the path towards Shakaland we could see this lake shining through the trees. It reminded me of Paul Simon's description of the Mississippi River in his lyrics to the song Graceland.

My wife Cathy and I were on a recce to decide whether we could live a life running a motor dealership in Empangeni. The night before we had stayed in the B&B of the Kramer's near Gingindhlovu. Brian is an accomplished pianist and had played for over an hour for us while we had dinner. We felt a little self-conscious as we were the only guests. The next morning they recommended we drive the circular route through the Nkwaleni valley to Empangeni.

So there we were, looking at the Goodetrouw dam, in the midst of a reconstructed Zulu village, still remembering the concert and superb meal of the previous evening; the whole experience had a surreal feel to it.

In that place we found the name for our business

There were exhibits of traditional Zulu culture and craft

at Shakaland. We had already decided that we would choose a Zulu name for our business if we settled on Empangeni for our future.

And there it was; an exhibit to the traditional herbal healer, the Inyanga.

My family had a holiday in the Inyanga mountains in eastern Zimbabwe when I was a boy. We stayed in a cottage in a pine forest just yards from a 2000 foot drop to the Pungwe river. I remember mist swirling in the forest in the morning and swimming in ice-cold rivers. It was a happy memory.

And it eventually became a happy name. I like to think there was a little intervention in us finding the name before we found the business.

Empangeni was a shock. Today I look at the familiar sights of the town with love, and it is hard to remember just how alienated we felt on that first visit.

It was a Saturday morning and thousands of people from the neighbouring districts had come shopping. The central business district was bedlam. Outside of the main shopping centre and a few banks the buildings were old single or double-storey structures. It wasn't too clean.

We called in at Mercron Motors, the Mercedes-Benz dealer which had been cancelled, although the staff knew nothing about it at the time of that visit. It had a dejected feel, as if it already knew its fate.

Although things looked not too promising we decided to at least investigate the property market while we were there. In an estate agency opposite the Sanlam Centre I asked a staff member who was the best commercial property man in town. She told me his name was John Vermaak and directed us to a building around the corner.

And so this larger than life man entered our lives. John

proved to be a wonderful friend of our business, specially in the formative times when we needed suppliers and customers. He and his wife Dawn had numerous dinner parties to which they invited people who were to become friends and customers. When we came to town we needed accommodation for a few months and stayed in the first room they completed in their new venture, the Amble Inn. Later he introduced me to Rotary.

On that first visit I could not give my name as I had to disclose that we wanted property for a motor dealership, and it would have been unfair on the staff of Mercron Motors if rumours started of them closing before they were properly informed by their owners.

John did his homework, and when I phoned him a few weeks later and said "I'm the guy who came to see you a few weeks ago", he answered "Hello Pete".

When we returned to our beautiful thatch-roofed home in Glen Austin after that first visit it was a relief, and we thought we would never see Empangeni again.

But fate had us by the scruff of the neck.

Chapter 3.

Starting from scratch.

We started with nothing.

I was persona non grata to the previous dealer, who could not really be blamed as in my capacity at Mercedes-Benz of SA I was party to the decision to cancel them.

It proved to be a blessing in the end as we would have attracted to ourselves their image in the community if we had used their facilities. The name change would not have been sufficient. Even with a change of name and premises we encountered angry customers who were aggrieved at the treatment they had received before.

Money, people and facilities. That's all we had to get together! Well, not quite, but those were the headlines.

Money was the one I underestimated the most and the principal reason for us taking six long years to start earning a positive return. We were badly undercapitalized and leased everything apart from some special tools, workshop equipment and office furniture.

I received what I believed to be a good severance package

from Mercedes-Benz, thinking it would cover around one-quarter of our funding requirements. In the end it barely covered ten percent. I also approached a friend who was to become my silent partner. He thought his family might be interested to take a share in the business, and they did. For many years the partnership was good for me and not for them. Happily, in the end they received value for the risk they took.

My partner helped us in our application for overdraft facilities at FNB, and his understanding of the banking requirements was invaluable. Local bank managers had some autonomy in those days and the Empangeni manager, Colin van Dyk was not afraid to use it. I was sad to lose him to the corporate division in Durban. He was not only a banker with courage; he was a fellow Rotarian and proposed me for Zululand Businessman of the Year far too early in the life of our business. I was flattered by his belief in us.

Finally the most important leg of a motor dealers' finances, floor plan facilities, were secured thanks to my long-standing relationship with Wesbank, and the trust of their senior managers, for I did not have the securities that would normally have been required.

John Vermaak found us the facilities, two 800 square metre steel buildings just completed and a 250 square metre showroom within walking distance.

Once the employees of the previous dealership knew of the developments we were free to announce ourselves through the media and advertise for staff. We were still living in Midrand, Johannesburg when the first and only ad appeared. It asked for applications in all positions for a new Mercedes-Benz dealer, opening in February 1995. At that time the only two staff members were my wife and I!

The telephone number in the ad was our home number in Midrand. I had bought a combination telephone and fax machine and was ready for calls when the newspaper came out. Within an hour the ring tone failed and I spent that first day picking up the phone every 30 seconds or so in case someone was on the line; in most cases that was so.

I cannot remember how many enquiries we received. Many we could screen immediately, but that still left around fifty people to interview and that number excluded the workshop staff that eventually came to us from the previous business, virtually en mass.

John offered the boardroom at Maxprop and we interviewed for several days into the early evening. We filled every position from that one ad. Two of the managers who were still with us when we sold the business 13 years later were hired that week; in fact we enjoyed tremendous loyalty from staff as half of the original complement of just over 30 people and four of the original five managers lasted the ride.

The most special person we hired was Cheryl Evans, our accountant. Cheryl had been the accountant for an auditing firm in Johannesburg, but she and her husband David made a decision to relocate to the coast in the interest of their daughter who had severe eye problems. Their decision was our good fortune; Cheryl became my second-in-command and we would never have survived our cash crunch years without her knowledge and sheer bloody-mindedness.

In January a few of us started preparing the facilities for opening. All of the suppliers; air conditioning; electrical work; office fittings; screenwriting and many more were recommended by John Vermaak. Only specialist suppliers to the motor industry like the people who installed hoists and parts shelving came from referrals from dealer friends.

We worked like dogs in the middle of a Zululand summer with temperatures in the two steel factories probably in the 40's. We used bricks laid out on the floor to determine the most efficient layout for the workshop. The parts department security consisted of a diamond mesh fence across a section of the building.

Not everything got finished. When the first cars arrived we did not have hoists and had to pre-deliver them on small trestles. The first parts shipment arrived before the shelving and had to be laid out on the floor in blue Mercedes-Benz boxes. Computers were delayed as was the system we adopted, Automate, and the first transactions were conducted on manual invoice books from the CNA.

Unfortunately we never kept a photographic record, but I have two special pictures in my mind. One was driving towards the facility early on a Saturday morning and seeing Chris Combrinck (who started as Parts Manager and later became Used Car Manager) driving ahead of me with his two young sons, also unable to stay away. The other is the state of Cheryl's chair. It was the only piece of furniture we had for weeks and everyone had their turn collapsing into it and dropping paint on it.

Such an enormously painful birth deserved to bear fruit in time.

CHAPTER 4.

Political violence, road accidents and taxi wars.

As you approach Empangeni from the north west you see a row of buildings standing in a line above the cane fields which look strangely like the ramparts of a walled city. At least that was my fanciful idea in my early days of doing business in the town.

The society in which we found ourselves was also reminiscent of life in a Rhodesian town; not very prosperous, male dominated and club orientated. Not great for a woman.

And of course the comparison is very much supported by the presence of nature everywhere you look. The north coast of KwazuluNatal is wild, not at all like the holiday and retirement village orientation of the infrastructure on the south coast.

In our first months of starting our business we found out just how wild.

In 1995 the war between the ANC and the Inkatha

Freedom Party still raged in Zululand. Societies and families were split, as were the places where people lived. Some of the older black suburbs remained loyal to the IFP which espoused traditional Zulu cultural values. Some of the newer suburbs had large numbers of migrant workers, many who had been living on the Reef, and they embraced the more modern urban values of the ANC.

There should have been space for both but the human landscape was marked by political intolerance, which was seen daily in the ungovernable municipal and regional forums, and murder for revenge and personal gain.

Many of our staff lived in the old tribal trust lands, their rustic homes widespread among the farmlands. A number of them told me that they slept in the bush for fear that their home would be raided and torched in the night.

This political and cultural reality made it difficult for us to choose a black partner. We could not afford to be seen to favour any one group of persons over another. In the end we found a wonderful woman, Sheila Ngubane, who embraced the best of all. Sheila was descended from the royal Zulu line; her husband Ben was an IFP member who rose to the premiership of KwazuluNatal but became a cabinet minister in the ANC government and eventually Ambassador to Japan. Sheila did outstanding work among rural women and was much loved in her community.

Despite the respect Sheila enjoyed by many I still had approaches from others trying to undermine her in order to promote their cause in becoming shareholders in Inyanga Motors. These suitors displayed the worst of the motives which drove many in the emerging black business community; the belief that they could enrich themselves on the back of government's black empowerment programmes without the need for hard work, experience or skill.

Nowhere is this form of economic intolerance more evident than in the taxi business. On more than one occasion the taxi ranks in Empangeni were the scene of gun battles which sometimes spilled over into other areas of town. The fight was about economic gain; taxi routes, parking privileges; decisions normally made around meeting tables not at the end of a gun.

I was befriended by a larger than life man called Mandla Buthelezi. We once helped him when his car broke down and he became a customer and we had a number of conversations over tea in my office. He once told me that the problem with black workers is that they left their brains outside the factory gate because they had been indoctrinated in the belief that they could not contribute.

Mandla ran a fleet of taxis and was also entering the bus market. He had an abundance of entrepreneurial talent. Somehow I always thought he would get into trouble because he was a dominating figure and I guessed that he did not tolerate competition. Nevertheless I was really saddened when he was gunned down in an ambush at an outlying filling station.

The worst violence in Zululand does not emanate from political intolerance or taxi wars; it is enacted on the roads. Taxis of course play the star role in this drama, but the extremely high rate of accident deaths can also be ascribed to poor training and vehicle maintenance, and to the magnification of these causes by crooked officials who take bribes to give false licences and roadworthy certificates.

I would estimate that a quarter to a third of the front page lead stories in the Zululand Observer concern road deaths and injuries. Often the front page picture shows bedlam strewn across one of our roads. I was invited by the newspaper to one of their internal critique sessions in which their editorial and advertising staffs discuss the most recent paper. I was surprised at their own depth of concern at the negative image portrayed by their coverage of road accidents; but the bottom line was that the most gruesome pictures sold the most papers; their editor received an award one year for his coverage of such matters.

Whilst at Mercedes-Benz I was invited to join the Drive Alive campaign (later changed to Arrive Alive). Our meetings were held at the offices of The Star newspaper in downtown Johannesburg. The campaign was driven by Moira Winslow who had lost family members in a crash caused by drag racing Porsche drivers on the N1 north of Pretoria. Most of our discussion was how to instil caution and good road habits into South African road users.

And from that point of view one would say that the coverage given to the subject by the Zululand Observer promotes a more careful approach. But I don't see the results.

A most poignant tragedy was the death of five young people travelling back from a Sharks rugby game at night. Their destination was the farm of one of their parents just south of the Tugela River. It is speculated that the driver missed the off-ramp which led to the farm and a few kilometres further fell asleep and crashed into the pylon of an overhead bridge.

As a memorial five Fever trees were planted on the embankment above the scene of the accident.

I wrote a poem about this tragedy. It is a poem of hope and I mean it to also be a message of hope for the positive resolution of the problems I have described in this chapter;

Five Trees

When you have lost, you are alone
but it needn't be so.

Near the Tugela
there are five trees planted in a row.

For many years their growth was stunted
as if the loss they represent
was too hard to bear.

But the other day I saw
them looking strong and healthy
as if the grief period was over.

And I had this thought
that beneath the soil on the bank
the roots must be holding hands.

No longer alone
forever friends.

Author's note; I wrote this chapter after I had completed the book to give a sense of the kind of world we had migrated to, and some of the issues which had a bearing on our work and play.

Chapter 5.

Building the brand Inyanga.

Most motor manufacturers don't want the dealer to have an identity.

They believe their brand should be paramount, and should be associated with a place name, as in Mercedes-Benz Empangeni, rather than a name that might compete with them, as in Cleary Mercedes-Benz.

They miss out on a huge opportunity.

Allowing the dealer to have an identity gives the motor brand a local face which can add to its attractiveness. Over time the local brand, the dealer, and the motor brand become a stronger entity. Unfortunately ego and lack of respect for dealer capability will never allow the motor manufacturers to see the marketing sense of this argument.

We were not going to miss the opportunity of building our dealership into a respected member of the local community and business environment, and that also required us to build our brand Inyanga.

The word Inyanga has several meanings in Zulu; as well

as the traditional healer, the meaning that first attracted us to the name; it also means the moon and is a day of the week. We asked locals, as well as language academics, if there were any negative connotations to the name and received only positive confirmation.

I asked D'Arcy to help us with a logo and graphic design. The moon was an obvious symbol which could be used as a unifying device in literature and signage. The moon was tricky because in its most recognisable form, the crescent, it is positively associated with the Muslim religion. The agency came up with a graphic which depicted a full yellow moon with clouds floating across its face.

To allow consumers to make the connection to this new, strange name the words Inyanga Motors ran with a sub line which read "Your local Mercedes-Benz, Honda and Colt dealer".

We ran with that design for a while but it was too fussy, and the logo type the agency included was designed by them and all printing required original artwork to duplicate it. Eventually we found a logotype similar to it and used that. The graphic was dropped.

It is an absurdity in South Africa that you are allowed to use superlatives but not comparatives in advertising. You can say "the best", but not "better than". We changed the sub line under our brand name to "Where you find the world's best cars and trucks"; fully expecting a local challenge but it never came. I was delighted because "best" is a word with strong connotations of quality and excellence.

We were fortunate to find that the local newspaper, the Zululand Observer, which was then published once a week, gave excellent coverage of our target markets and was an important source of local news. I was irritated that they gave us a credit limit of only R5000, barely enough to pay for one full-page ad. For all I know our limit is still R5000 although our annual advertising spend is more than a million rand today.

The first ad we ran had the headline "A new moon is rising over Zululand" Not one of our best efforts. I used a very ego-centric device; I signed the ads with my name. I figured that the brand was synonymous with the owners, my wife Cathy and I, and people should know us, and feel they could approach us directly when we failed them. And they did.

It was an excellent strategy and the community knew who we were in a very short time. I was often amused that, even when my name hadn't appeared in the paper for some time, customers would say "Oh, I saw you in the Observer the other day".

We started to run ads that talked about our differences. When we decided to give buyers a full tank of fuel on delivery of their new vehicle (not a common practice in those days) the ad said "When you buy a car from us you can drive to the ends of the province, and not just around the corner"

A customer complained to me that he had been overcharged for a part. I checked and he had. We ran the story in an ad "We overcharged a customer the other day" We were the first to provide emergency breakdown service and ran an ad with a road map of northern Natal and a line that explained that our technicians knew this territory well.

A Porsche owner who I met socially told me his dealer in Durban could not fix his car. We had a youngster in our workshop who was good with engines and I offered to have a go on his car. We fixed the car and ran an ad "A strange story about a Porsche and a Mercedes-Benz dealer"

And we were sure to take a tilt at ourselves. When

Mercedes-Benz came out with a new C-Class diesel model Cathy and I took it on a drive to Durban. I measured the fuel consumption on the trip down and told Cathy, she then noticed I had the car in fifth, and hadn't realized that the car had a new 6-speed transmission. The ad told of a clever car and a dumb driver.

We were the first dealer to run full-page ads in the paper, and that really got people to sit up and take notice. It was regarded as nothing short of outrageous, particularly by our fellow dealers who now had to match our exposure.

Another way in which we personalized Inyanga Motors was the telephone messages when you phoned in and were put on hold. The company offering the on hold service also provided a scripting service and had professional readers. We didn't use those services; I wrote the messages and went down to their studio in Durban around once a quarter to personally record them.

Our message to the community was clear; this is our business; we are personally responsible; we are fallible but will do everything we can to fix your problem; we want this to be an outstanding business for our customers and our staff.

Chapter 6.

The facility fiasco.

I don't know how I signed such a dumb contract with the landlord of our first workshops. It was to have enormous cost implications.

The contract period was one year with an option for a further three months. In that short time we had to find a developer, a site for the business and get the dealership built which was plain ridiculous.

The landlord played games with us. He would only extend the lease period at more than double the rental. He had an alternative tenant who would pay this amount which was a lie; the building stood empty for more than a year after we vacated it. Hardus Venter, who was the lead man in the consortium which was developing our new dealership, went down to Durban to personally try to talk sense into the man, without success.

Pride got the better of rational judgment and I decided to move the business. In retrospect staying where we were until our new building was completed was probably the most economic option.

We found an old building on Ngwelezane Road that had been designed for a carpentry business. The best you could say for it was that it was larger than the premises we were vacating, and the location was a marginal improvement. Our managers were horrified at my optimism and the way I minimized the difficulties. I took each one to the site and we planned together where their department would be located and what changes were required.

The changes were extensive; the front two sections had to be tiled, new offices needed to be built, additional lighting was needed, the building had to have computer cables installed, toilets needed to be upgraded, and air conditioning had to be installed in the showrooms and offices (at least we were able to transfer the air conditioning from one building to the next and there are still some units in Inyanga that survived three moves).

In the midst of our greatest difficulties there is always an opportunity for humour if you look out for it. The main showroom had a raised wooden office in the one corner which was to be Cathy's office as the manager of that department. It soon became known as the Baywatch Booth, a compliment to the appearance of the office and its occupant!

It was much more fun taking the managers and staff on inspection visits to our new premises as they neared completion. They could see that the hardships they had suffered were about to be rewarded.

The Inyanga Motors premises are part of a development at the eastern entrance to Empangeni, on the corner of John Ross Highway and Impala Road. It remains one of the best motor dealer sites in Zululand with passing traffic of almost twenty thousand vehicles a day. It has a grand location, is one of the best-looking buildings in town and has a grand name, Inyanga Plaza

CHAPTER 7.

Learning the hard way.

Learning by your mistakes is an easy thing to say, but a hard thing to have to go through.

I had visited dealers in many parts of the world; I'd visited and advised dealers in South Africa, I'd worked for Eastvaal Ford. None of that was the real thing.

When we started the business our auditor Theo de Kooker, a very astute businessman, said to me diffidently "the secret to retail is control Peter. But you know that". I wish I had. Theo is still giving me good advice, and I'm a better listener today.

I'm going to mention a few of the bigger mistakes we made. It's not easy to even write about them.

The first big one was six tippers we traded in from a transport company called Oosthuizens in our second year of operation. The salesman who appraised the vehicles at the mine where they were operating was not experienced. He wrote down a description of each of the vehicles, but there remains a suspicion that the vehicles that arrived at our yard were different. We eventually sold the last of those trucks two years later.

The lessons learnt; trucks are not to be traded unless you have expertise; salespeople cannot be trusted to be objective if they can gain from the deal; when you know you've got a problem get rid of it fast and take the knock; when you're uncertain use the profit of the new vehicle to write back the used vehicle.

Used cars and trucks caused the biggest individual financial losses. At the heart of the problem is placing trust in the wrong people and lack of control. Both of these can be laid at my door.

In the beginning the stars in our business in my eyes were the people doing the selling. I didn't want them overly controlled. When it came to a decision between the two approaches I always erred on behalf of making the sale. That is a very risky thing to do and much of the reason for doing it was to try to get the company into the black; if the two first controllers in our business, Cheryl Evans and Cathy had run the show we would have started to make money years earlier.

We went through the big bang before used vehicles came right. One of our used managers was well intentioned and honest but did not have control of his salesmen or his stock. His strategy was to sell all brands of cars from cheap to medium priced, and the sales volumes were high. But so too were the stock levels, the reconditioning costs and the comeback cost.

One of his salesmen was rolling deposits, pocketing the deposit and using the next one for the earlier sale and so on. Cars were also going in and out of stock to customers. When it was discovered it was a huge mess and it caused a parting of company for the sales manager. The sales person was charged for criminal offences, arrested and mysteriously disappeared.

We had to get rid of close to 100 cars, and quickly as the lack of cash flow was killing us.

I sought the help of Peter Azzie and he introduced me to Lee Martin, a wholesale operator in Durban who was later to become a business partner. Lee used her contacts to organize an auction which was to be held on the Empangeni cricket club field. Lee persuaded the auctioneer to accept a flat fee, and she publicized the auction.

The event started disastrously; one of the cars was in an accident being driven to the venue and was badly damaged; it rained on the Saturday of the auction and we didn't know if the buyers would come from Durban in that weather.

It turned out a great success and we sold over 80 cars.

We lost one million rand in one day, but we saved the company. That sounds Dutch but if we had not freed up the R5 million tied up in stock the company would have been unable to trade.

We never got into trouble with used cars again. Chris Combrinck, one of our original managers was transferred from parts to used cars and he became a good used car practitioner. He erred on the side of conservatism and I often pushed him to grow his department, but if I had to choose today, I'd always take the conservative safe approach with used cars.

My least favourite customers are truck operators. I don't know what it is with that industry because the cost of entry is high, but it seems to attract an inordinate number of chancers. One of these was a man who ran trucks out of Richards Bay.

We had sold him a number of Actros models and that particular truck model had problems with radiator fans causing excessive downtime. So, in a way, Mercedes-Benz was party to the customer's problem. He could not pay his truck repair bills and owed us over R100 000.

I went to see him. He made me an offer; he had won a new contract and needed to buy more trucks, if he bought our trucks would we write off part of the debt. I phoned Geoff du Plessis, Management Board Member for Commercial Vehicles and asked if he would contribute and we agreed to share a portion of the debt.

I told him he had a deal if he would sign an offer to purchase on the new trucks. He signed and when the trucks came he reneged on the deal.

Large truck fleets can be even more of a problem because they have enormous pull with the manufacturer and use that power to give the dealer heartache. We had an interesting truck operation being run by Unitrans for Richards Bay Minerals.

Mercedes-Benz trucks were being used to pull a road train of ore weighing 150 tonnes. This was a critical mass and required careful maintenance because of the strain on the drivetrain. It was also a dirty operation because of the fine ore which entered filter systems and damaged wiring looms.

There were plenty of problems and large repair bills were run up. Unitrans blamed Mercedes-Benz for truck selection and argued these repairs should be handled under the warranty terms. Mercedes-Benz sent engineers to investigate and blamed Unitrans maintenance procedures. We were in the middle. Our bills did not get paid by either party and sometimes ran to more than R300 000.

Today the brands that I sell have no heavy truck models, and I couldn't be happier.

CHAPTER 8.

Trying to grow our way out of trouble.

We studied our management cost accounts and could not see a way out of the hole by cutting costs.

We came to the conclusion we had to grow the business while holding costs.

It was the wrong strategy. We should have tried harder. The new ventures we embraced only dug the hole deeper.

The first one we tried was SsangYong.

The introduction came from Terry Gregory who had worked for me at Mercedes-Benz of South Africa. Two investors, both with no previous motor experience, had obtained the franchise from the Korean company. They hired Terry as their general manager and he was looking for dealers.

It seemed to be a good fit. The vehicle had Mercedes-Benz engines and I had actually seen one of their models, the Musso, in the engineering parking lot in Stuttgart. In South Africa, in defiance of their license agreement with Mercedes-

Benz, the distributors placed stickers in the rear windows proclaiming "Powered by Mercedes-Benz".

I phoned my partner from the Ghost Mountain Inn, where we were having a budget meeting with our managers, and asked his opinion. He was sceptical but supported the need to grow.

It did not cost much to start the franchise, but every rand turned out to be a rand wasted. We hired some empty shops in Inyanga Plaza, turned them into a showroom, put up the signage and bought a limited number of special tools and spare parts. We were to service the vehicles in our Inyanga workshop.

The SsangYong Musso had quality problems unfortunately, mainly with the gearbox and the hydraulic 4WD system. I say unfortunately because it offered excellent value, comfort and roominess and the promise of the Mercedes-Benz engine was a draw card.

Sales volumes remained below the critical level at which you can hire good salespeople who can make a decent living selling that brand. In my experience that level is ten vehicles a month.

My business partner was keen that we obtain a franchise for a cheaper brand and we settled on Daewoo. The idea was to take an additional shop next to SsangYong, break down the walls between the two and have the sales team sell both brands. None of the models offered by the two brands were in direct competition with one another.

Daewoo also wasn't a good choice. New in South Africa, the distributors lacked the necessary infrastructure. Spare parts were a headache. The cars themselves were of a decent technical standard but the build quality was poor. Today they are being sold under the Chevrolet brand name in South Africa and doing well.

I'm sure by now you are confused at the geography of Inyanga Plaza and how we could take "additional shops". Inyanga Motors was the anchor tenant in this development, and had the prime showroom positions at the corner of John Ross and Impala Road. Flanking Inyanga Motors, and running parallel to the two roads were seven line shops along the John Ross arm and six along the Impala Road arm.

The developers were never successful at attracting tenants, which was our good fortune because it allowed us to expand. Eventually we leased the entire complex when we moved our parts department into the building along the Impala Road flank

Before that happened we took two more shops and turned them into a fitment centre for automotive products. One of our young technicians showed interest and capability in the electronics field. We gave him the opportunity to develop a business specializing in alarm and sound systems for cars. We didn't support him properly, and maybe gave him too much leeway; a management style of mine which often paid off, but not this time.

In retrospect we were clutching at straws. Unable to shrink the business in any meaningful way we looked to grow it. In the end the three ventures in this chapter just made it worse and were eventually abandoned.

Although we didn't know it at the time we had reached the lowest point in the fortunes of the company. But first a tragedy in another country had to take place to give us a fuller understanding of our role in this life.

Chapter 9.

Finding our soul.

Often in life change is triggered by a single event. It happened at Ford when a personality test in New Orleans made me realise I had lost my identity. And it happened to us in 2000 when an accident in Mozambique made us question our priorities.

We travelled in two vehicles; Cathy's brother Alan Armstrong, his wife Jenny, son Duncan and a friend in one vehicle and Cathy and I, Andrew and Susan in the other.

The holiday was jinxed from the start. No sooner had we entered Mozambique territory when Alan's vehicle started playing up. Then on the second morning we missed the convoy time to cross the Limpopo River. No-one in the tented camp had told us that the flood damage had taken out the main bridge across the Limpopo at Shai Shai and that there was a detour to the west which could only be traversed once a day from the north and once from the south.

We were confronted by armed militia in a small town and decided to go around the town through the flooded fields. It was hectic and frightening. North of the Limpopo there was a lack of fuel as the replenishment vehicles were not getting through. I ended up towing Alan's vehicle for 30 kilometres until we found a supply of diesel.

It was a low point for Alan who's much vaunted Land Cruiser was being towed by a Colt bakkie!

On the road home we travelled alone. The Armstrong's wanted to stay another day and we made the decision to stick to our original schedule. We left in the dark to reach the Limpopo crossing with the southbound convoy at first light. Cathy took over the driving duties and just south of the river, and some 25 kilometres from Macia, an approaching driver tried to avoid a pothole and lost control of his vehicle causing us to unavoidably hit them.

We were fortunate to end up in a mission station run by Willem Nel, a young man of quiet determination and incredible wisdom. And a deep love of God.

When we returned we were changed people. The incident had stripped us of a lifetime of defences; we could have been killed by the angry mob at the accident scene had it not been for a bystander who explained in language we could not understand that the other driver was to blame; Cathy would have been jailed until the court hearing but for Willem; I slept on the ground and we ate from the humble communal bowl.

We had been totally reliant on others and they had pulled us through. It was time to acknowledge our gratitude to God and we found a church community in Mtunzini which has been near the centre of our lives since then. Gratitude and community has replaced self-centred absorption and all of our relationships have deepened and become more satisfying since then.

Seven years later we returned to Mozambique. We thought we would never again put ourselves into potential danger, but our daughter Caryn was keen to purchase a property in Tofu and we agreed to accompany her. Once again we made the mistake of travelling alone.

Just six kilometres from our intended overnight destination we were pulled over by armed civilian police and the nightmare started again. A call to the owners of the inn caused some consternation to our tormentors and they released us. (In a follow-up operation one of the two civilian police who had illegally accosted us shot at the son of the innkeeper and the weapon misfired).

That night I went into the bathroom in the early hours of the morning and wrote this poem;

Sometimes you see eternity.

Face swollen, shouting
Demanding ridiculous sums of money
For the trivial offence
Threatening jail if we don't pay his bribe.

The other one, standing near
Not speaking
But no less threatening with his AK47.

Welcome to Mozambique.

I am reminded of an earlier time
Moments of terrifying vulnerability
Not 100 kilometres from this place.

It was the time the Limpopo flooded
Washing away the main bridge
Reducing passage to lesser roads

Restricted to one convoy a day.

We foolishly sought a way with a guide
Around the military-controlled town
A dreadful journey through barely seen
And barely passable mud tracks
Past settlements from an earlier civilization.

And when the tension eased
And we were almost through
The soldier running up the embankment with his rifle.

We did not stop
We had just had enough of that fearful place
We drove through
Our offence too small for him to shoot.

The incident spoilt our holiday
Always present the lurking fear
Of the journey back through that place.

And as it so often happens, the danger came not there
But further on
Beyond the floodplains of the Limpopo.

A lone approaching car lost control
And met us sideways in the road.

The noise of the impact was shocking
Our car reared up
It's nose came to rest on the roadside bank.

After that tearing, screaming noise
An utter silence
And then tentative exploring hands to see if we were hurt

Our good fortune was not shared
By the two men and the woman in the other car
Their battered bodies lay entombed for hours
Before help arrived.

Help came in the form of interrogation,
Negotiation
It seemed endless with no hope.

Somehow we arrived at a small police station
On the shaded streets of a nearby provincial town.

They let us walk to the hospital
Sympathetic to our fears for our children
Who had been taken there earlier.

The hospital was a shell
In one room the woman from the other car,
Placed on a bare table, squatting on her broken hip
Her eyes unseeing from the endless pain.

They told us our son and daughter
Had been taken by the missionary
They did not know the extent of their injuries
Only that one or maybe two men had died.

Back at the police station
We were finally found
By the gentle man of God, bringing our children
Bandaged, but alive.

He worked another miracle
In his quiet deferential way
He persuaded the police
To release us into his custody.

His custody the mission station
He had founded
In the coastal bush outside that town,

There we spent some days
Sharing their spartan meals
Admiring their devotion and simplicity
Laying our bruised bodies to rest
On the concrete floor at night.

In that place we found ourselves for the future
The dreadful events opening our hearts
Bringing the peace and hope
Of something much larger than ourselves.

Sometimes, if you are lucky
You do not die.

Sometimes, if you are lucky
You see eternity.

Adversity can bring out the best in us. And it can stimulate creativity. On that second trip to Mozambique I wrote three poems, two included in this chapter, and "My African Ancestor" which is included in the Ford Motor Company section.

On our return trip we stopped for the night in Willem and Carol's mission. Much progress had been made, with many more students and buildings. They now even have tunnels in which they grow vegetables. I was glad that my tithe to them for the last seven years had contributed to something so encouraging.

The next morning, before sunrise, I walked through the bush to a nearby community well which always had crowds of villagers around it in daylight hours. The light was poor for photography but I did get a shot down the well with the aid of flash. It is pleasing to me that after the violence of our experiences in Mozambique, and the violence in the "eternity" poem, I was able to write something more gentle;

The well near Volta a Biblia.

I'm looking at my photograph of the well
I'm looking at the lining of worn slick stones
I'm looking at the shine on the water below.

It is the grey before dawn
But already the clear high voices all around
Announce the first of many, many visits.

If I could hide my camera in this tree
And take a time sequence of one whole day
What an extraordinary record that would be.

I see a similar picture far to the west
Animals on a wagon-wheel of narrow tracks
Converging silently on the waterhole.

But oh, how much more colour and meaning
In the ebb and flow of the women and children
At the well, near Volta a Biblia.

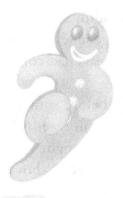

CHAPTER 10.

With a little help from my friends.

One of the reasons for us eventually starting to trade profitably was that we applied what we learnt in performance groups.

A performance group is a number of dealers of similar size or composition meeting periodically, usually three or four times a year, to compare financial results and learn from one another.

The concept was started in the US and brought to South Africa by Paddy O'Brien, a most remarkable man and a most remarkable teacher. Paddy made his name introducing the Toyota Touch programme for Brand Pretorius and then obtained the franchise for the British dealer training company Sewells, and joined forces with Wesbank.

I was eventually to be a part of three performance groups, but none more satisfying than the first group of relatively small Natal independent dealers. The core group comprised two Mercedes-Benz dealers, the other being Harvey Kelly's business in Kokstad, two VW dealers, one from our town and one from Durban, a Nissan dealer from Durban, a Delta dealer from Newcastle and a Toyota dealer with several branches on the South Coast.

What made this performance group particularly successful was that most of us had family in our businesses and they became involved in the group, in a learning and fellowship sense.

The style of this group was to gather the day before the meeting so that we could have a meal together and renew our comradeship. We rotated the meetings so that we all had a turn being the host and presenting our business for inspection and comment.

Eventually, as much as I loved the company of those dealers, I was taking home fewer and fewer ideas and Paddy suggested I join a group of large metropolitan dealers. This group never had the fellowship I had enjoyed previously; there were too many professional managers from large dealer groups, some of whom did not want to be there, there were too many changes, and Paddy did not run it personally.

Nevertheless that group offered plenty of opportunity to learn new ways of doing business. I was particularly taken with the flair of Colin Lazarus, whose Ford dealership in Pretoria must be one of the best in the world in its attractiveness, customer handling processes and way of preserving the individual identities of a number of brands in one facility.

We had some moments too, none more memorable than taking off from Bloemfontein airport in a howling gale in Colin's small twin-engine plane.

My final group offered probably the best opportunity to learn because it comprised of only DaimlerChrysler market centre dealers. A market centre is a category of dealer which offered all of the brands in the DaimlerChrysler stable. We insisted that Paddy run that group personally which meant we had to fit in with his hectic schedule of managing his new business ventures in Australia and South-East Asia.

There were some dealers in that group who knew how to make money. Whilst the average amongst us managed a return on sales of around 2,5 to 3,0%, there were three dealers who made in excess of 5%.

It was interesting that they had similar characteristics; they were tightly controlled businesses, their dealer principals, or their owners had an accounting background and they had unattractive and old facilities. The conclusion was simple; they ran their businesses to make money and not to reflect the ambitions of the manufacturer.

There were two other incidents in which Paddy O'Brien featured prominently in the life of our business.

When we were going through our tough and unprofitable times DaimlerChrysler asked Paddy to do an analysis of whether he felt we could survive. He gave them such a glowing report that Theo Swanepoel, the dealer development manager, said to me later "that man really likes you".

We invited Paddy to attend one of our quarterly budget meetings. I always tried to introduce something new in these meetings and Paddy tried an intervention which did not really work, but out of which came this dream of creating a business of very special appeal.

He called us the "Jewel of the North".

CHAPTER 11.

Community affairs.

I was sitting in a Rotary meeting listening to this dedicated young British woman talking about eye cataract operations. I was struck by the wonder of it; one day you were blind and the next you could see!

So began the first of our successful community projects.

The woman was Liz Moulton and she was the local organizer for an international NGO called Vision 20/20. I invited her to meet with myself and a small group of our managers who I knew would want to be involved, chief among them being my wife Cathy.

Out of that meeting came a number of principles which were to guide us in other ventures. The contact person had to be personally involved, there had to be accountability and transparency and we had to involve customers and staff.

The device we used to involve customers was to give Vision 20/20 a fixed amount per vehicle sold in the month. That way we could say to customers that they were personally contributing towards someone regaining their sight.

Liz managed the money we gave to her organization exceptionally well, reporting to us the balance of the fund and obtaining our approval for expenditure. In the beginning the funds were spent buying the lenses placed in the eye by the surgeons because they were not affordable to the patients. Later, when government started providing the lenses, our funds paid for air conditioners in the eye clinic at Ngwelezane hospital and eventually the building of a special ward for recovering patients.

Cathy and I were struck by the dedication and humbleness of the two surgeons at the Ngwelezane hospital. Neither was South African; the one was a young Belgian, the other a middle-aged Indian. Their salaries were small and we knew that their counterparts in private practice could afford to buy expensive sports cars from us.

We had the privilege to watch a cataract operation being performed, watching through a special training microscope which gave us the same view as the surgeon had. It was such a delicate operation to insert the lens.

Our drivers got involved in picking up patients from the rural areas. Unfortunately elderly blind people were not being brought forward by their families who did not want to lose their disability grants. Liz's people would go to pension pay stations, identify the patient and make arrangements to pick them up at a designated place.

It was almost a clandestine operation and we were nervous about our drivers going into some unsafe places; they were prepared to take the risk as they got such reward from picking up those old people the next day when they could see through their new eye and taking them home to see their families for the first time in years.

When we bought the Mercedes-Benz dealership in Vryheid

we started looking for a community project which we could help. Soon an excellently prepared proposal came to us for an orphanage in the town called Inkululeko Babies Home. It was run by Darleen and Danie van Tonder from a building attached to the church where Danie was the pastor. Craig Schnell checked it out for us when he was visiting Vryheid and gave a glowing report.

The next visit I paid to Vryheid I went to see the home. I was accompanied by Cheryl Evans and Eva Jansen. There we met this energetic little bundle of human compassion.

Darlene showed us the children, the facilities, the records they kept of the children for a potential adoption, the children's lockers, pictures of the children who had passed through their hands and been successfully adopted, children who had died. She knew every baby past and present and she talked, and talked and talked. Cheryl and Eva and I did not dare look at each other for fear of showing our emotion.

We hadn't gone two blocks from the orphanage before we had decided we were going to help, and how much per vehicle sold we would donate. We had none of us seen love given so unconditionally.

Inkululeko Babies Home soon became Cathy's favourite and she developed a friendship with Darlene. They had a problem with the babies who were not adopted and had a dream to build, alongside the baby's home, a home for the toddlers. Their church congregation prayed for a solution and one came. They were donated one million rand by Dettol to buy another house, and soon found one within walking distance. While they were renovating it they took the toddlers there frequently to acclimitise them to their new home and the toddlers soon referred to it as the Yellow House.

This is a different challenge for Darlene and Danie,

looking after children into adulthood and we hope they have the patience, wisdom and love, and the help of God, to see them through.

Cathy was becoming the driving force behind our community projects and the next one she picked up at a meeting of the Business Women's Association.

It was called Simunye Community Tourism, and was an organization developed in the rural communities near Lake Sibaya. The aim was to recruit and train staff from the rural areas for the many lodges which are developing around the game parks and conservation areas in northern Zululand. One of the services they ran was a booking office for tourists.

We met their energetic and charming organizer, Richard Mabaso and worked out a programme of assistance in which we purchased a years membership of Simunye for each new customer. The membership gave our customers discounts to the lodges and the KZN Game Parks.

Richard brought his boss to us for a meeting. Dr. Andrew Venter is the chairman of an umbrella organization called The Wildlands Conservation Trust, which has a number of projects, the most successful being Trees For Life. Richard, Andrew, Cathy and I had a meeting which Cathy later said was one of the most stimulating she had attended.

Andrew is committed and enthusiastic about his work and I was most taken with the Trees For Life story, where they facilitate the growing of indigenous trees in underprivileged schools and communities to bring income to people who have nothing. By the end of the meeting I had offered to give them free of rent a railway house in a complex we had obtained to expand our motor business. And I offered without thinking to refurbish the house not realizing the cost would be in excess of R100 000.

We had long heard of this amazing woman Bev Dunn who couldn't turn away children in trouble and made space for them in the homes she had been donated from Spoornet, next to the old railway station in Gingingdlovu.

A few of us went to visit her and found a distracted busy woman trying to hold things together for over forty children, as well as run a pre-school. One of the houses, not much more than 100 sq meters, housed the children; boys in one room, girls in the other and a bathroom in between.

There was a new house that they were turning into another dormitory but it was on the old railway station next to a pedestrian bridge where drunken men crossed to a nearby tavern. The house could not be used until proper security was arranged; in the meantime Bev had made a plan; she persuaded the ambulance service to use it as a base for their operation.

We decided on a different approach for our assistance. I believe in the credo that you need to give to receive and I wanted our staff to have the opportunity to reap the rewards that come with an act of compassion. We were going to ask them to make a monthly pledge of between R10 and R100 which the company would double.

We had pictures taken of each child at Bev's home and I did presentations to the staff in which I showed a picture of the child and described that child's difficult story. I did not get through a single presentation dry eyed. The staff responded magnificently, even the poorest of our people making a pledge of some money.

We met another outstanding person through tragic circumstances. One of our technicians lived in a rented house on a farm just outside Empangeni. On a weekend night he and his wife were entertaining another Inyanga couple when thieves broke into the house and held them at gun point. Deon tried to protect his wife, thinking they were going to harm her, and he was shot dead.

I was introduced to Larry Erasmus who ran Farm Watch, a private organization formed by a consortium of farmers to provide protection for their isolated homesteads and staff.

Larry's people found the murderers.

We made a long-term loan to Larry of a 4WD Colt bakkie to assist in their protection duties on the proviso that our customers and our technicians on emergency breakdowns would also fall into the ring of protection offered by Farm Watch.

It worked like this; our two service managers could call Larry's organization directly if a customer had broken down in a dangerous area and Farm Watch would travel to the site to protect the occupants of the vehicle, and our technicians, until the vehicle was repaired or the occupants moved to safety.

We provided another programme of assistance to the Bay Hospital, one which gave our staff a great deal of satisfaction. Periodically we would take terminally ill patients, including groups of children on visits to the Game Reserves, or for a boat cruise on Lake St. Lucia.

Our role was to provide the vehicles, usually Chrysler Voyagers, and the drivers. Bay Hospital provided the food and refreshments. Our staff members who did the driving duties or who accompanied the group never failed to rave about the wonder of seeing the gratitude of the patients, many of whom had never seen animals in the wild.

We shamelessly publicized our involvement in these community projects. We always sought opportunities for coverage in the local newspaper and always provided coverage in our own publication "Inyanga Diary", where the back page was headed "Helping Others".

Of course part of our motivation was positive publicity for our company, but more than that we were witnessing to a value of community responsibility, and encouraging our staff and customers to do likewise.

When I was named Businessman of the Year for 2000 by the Zululand Chamber it was a further endorsement of the broader role we took in the community.

Chapter 12.

Having fun.

I woke up in complete darkness in a room full of men. It was a very large room and all around I could hear the noises of sleep, and there was a moment of confusion. Then I remembered, this was our first Boy's Weekend at the Mthiyane Beach Camp, and this was our first night of the weekend.

I made my way out of the room with the help of a pencil light. Outside it was cool and doused with moonlight through the thin cloud cover. I passed the camp site where earlier Chris had cooked fish they caught butterfly style, drenched with butter and garlic, and Laity had serenaded us with his high voice and guitar.

I walked up the small dune to where I could see and hear the white breakers. Earlier the stronger boys had entertained themselves leaping out of moving bakkies to catch ghost crabs. They would not be so smart in the morning.

I sat there thinking of this strange company we were developing. In the midst of our unprofitable years around 30 of us, of all race groups, were having fellowship together in a very rough camp, the only accommodation some of the staff could afford.

From the beginnings of Inyanga Motors we believed in celebrating success and socialising together. I believe teamwork is based on trust, and trust comes from knowing your fellow worker, knowledge you gain from work interactions but also from swapping stories in a social environment.

Shortly after we moved to Inyanga Plaza I was approached to provide funds for materials to build a pub. The area chosen was a dead area flanked by a disused municipal electricity switch station and the steel walls of the truck wash bay. In one weekend a bunch of the staff erected a structure with a high peaked metal roof, gum pole supports and walls on two sides for privacy.

We named it Pete's Club, my dig at the extraordinary importance given by the local community to the various clubs in town. Later the name changed to Pete's pub.

The downside of a pub is the few who use it as a refuge to escape their other life. And we had that. The upside comes if you are prepared to put a little money and lots of organization into using the facility for team building.

The best of such usage at Inyanga Motors were our theme evenings.

Every quarter one of the departments had to put on a theme evening. The venue was Pete's pub and we provided food and the first few drinks free for all the staff. Later families could join and I always delighted at the kids playing in the truck workshop which must have been heaven for their enquiring minds.

Music had to be provided. There was a tradition of dancing on the bar counter and new employees were strongly encouraged to take a turn. The instigators of this frenetic activity were Cheryl Evans, our accountant, my wife Cathy and some of the younger set.

Some of the themes were memorable, none more so than the two I remember being staged by the Truck Workshop, the one an arm-wrestling machine they made, the other a mechanical bull which was a great hit with the competitive guys in the two workshops.

Pete's pub was also the venue we used for our Christmas parties which were always preceded by an awards ceremony where I had the opportunity to thank and reward the best performers and departments for the year.

The biggest and best parties were the three we had to celebrate our Dealer of the Year wins. DaimlerChrysler provided funds for these events and many of their senior managers attended. Their money was not enough for an Inyanga celebration and we generally spent double the allocation.

The DaimlerChrysler people always had a ball at our parties and were knocked out by the informality, the sheer fun of the events, and the comradeship across racial lines. I remember Fritz van Olst, then Board Member for Marketing, dancing with Fikile, our most fluid dancer, with this totally bemused look on his face.

If you're wondering why your company doesn't behave like this I have an answer for you; you don't have enough women in management.

Chapter 13.

Alan Ross.

Allister Richie phoned me and asked if he could come around and show me a car. He would not be drawn on the reason for this strange request.

Allister and I had known each other since the Ford days when, as Field Operations Manager, I had called on his dealership in Empangeni. We had renewed our friendship when I came to town and were serving on Rotary together at the time of the call.

The car was a Daihatsu Charade and it was surprisingly roomy and nippy for a small automatic.

The deal was that Ford had asked Ritchie Ford to dispose of the Daihatsu franchise, and would I take it, he was happy to give me the signage and special tools. I said no thanks; we had tried other franchises with negative results. He asked me to at least meet Alan Ross, the general manager of Daihatsu for Associated Motor Holdings, the import arm of the Imperial group.

Alan is a no-nonsense type of guy with a drive to succeed

and grow. He was not taking a rejection from me and before our first meeting was over he was peering into one of the vacant shops at Inyanga Plaza, pronouncing it to be perfect and phoning my landlord to negotiate a favourable lease.

We lucked out on someone to run the tiny business. Janene Beattie and her husband had owned one of the motorcycle businesses in town and their marriage had come to an end, as had their business. Janene had the experience of running all aspects of a small motor business, from administration to sales. She had three sons to provide for.

We sold more Daihatsu's in the first year than they did in Durban, a market ten times the size of ours. And we made half a million rand net profit, the first of our associated ventures to turn a profit.

Alan phoned me a year later and said they were impressed with our Daihatsu sales; did we want the Renault franchise? I said we would love to have Renault but we could not afford it. Rubbish, he said it won't cost you much and we can sort out those details later.

So we got the Renault franchise for a capital investment of less than R200 000 and moved into the next two vacant shops alongside Daihatsu. The two franchises, by then a separate company named DAU Motor Holdings, did fairly well in profit and sales, still managed by Janene.

In 2000 the Hyundai empire of Billy Rautenbach collapsed. Rautenbach had exploited a loophole of the local content programme, aided by government's desire to help their neighbour, to bring cars into Botswana, do very little assembly on them and bring them into South Africa at prices substantially lower than the local market. His cars were free of the many duties and costs imposed on South African made cars.

He had also built a chain of dealerships owned by his company and they had a refreshing approach to customer service. I knew of some of these ideas as a friend of mine, a commercial property developer, had quoted to build a dealership in Richards Bay for them. He sought and ignored my advice, which was don't touch them, they will be bankrupt in no time.

The developer is Mervyn Wallace and luckily he ignored my advice because we now lease that building, and all others around it.

Imperial bought the Hyundai assets from the liquidators and I got a call from Alan.

"Peter" he said, "I've been given the Hyundai mess to sort out and I'm going to make it work. Its payback time for you; I want you to take over the dealership in Richards Bay".

This one we truly could not afford, but you cannot say no to a man like Alan Ross. He finds a way to make it happen for you. In this instance, much of the equipment had been moved out of Richards Bay to a warehouse in Pinetown near Durban.

Alan gave me the name of his agent in Durban and I met with him on a Saturday and identified the equipment and office furniture that we needed. Everything in that dealership; hoists, special tools, parts shelving, desks, computers and manuals was provided.

Re-opening those Hyundai dealerships was hell. Customers were angry and the staff had been through months of uncertainty and worry. We lost heavily for two years before it came right and we are glad we hung in there, because it has been a South African success story.

The three brands that Alan brought to us, Daihatsu,

Renault and Hyundai form the core of our remaining business, described in the last chapter of the book.

Thanks Alan.

CHAPTER 14.

Building trust and confidence.

Never lie to your staff. Be as honest with your customers as they allow you to be.

Is this a motor dealer talking, and what's the sleight of hand in that second sentence? Let me answer the customer statement first; some customers lie to you. Luckily for us and our belief in human nature they are in the minority.

But some lie about the price they received from another dealer about the trade-in offer, they lie about their service history, and they sometimes even lie about the year of registration of their car. When money is involved morality gets worn a little thin around the edges. They usually trip themselves up and we pretend not to notice to let them save face.

When a customer plays it straight, so do we.

We always told our staff the bad news. I remember when I told our managers that I was going to tell the staff in my first address that we were losing money I got an almost violent response from Cheryl Evans. "You can't do that", she said.

"This is a small town and word will get out. No-one will give us credit".

Now, I have the greatest respect for Cheryl, but I have a fundamental belief that employees have the right to know how their company is doing. Perhaps it comes from the early days at Ford when my morale and belief in the company was so badly dented when they retrenched and tripped themselves up in lies.

Of course the investor has the most to lose because he cannot extricate himself from a bad situation easily; but people who work for you are investing their time in your company and your fortunes are also theirs.

We told the staff we were losing money and nobody stopped giving us credit.

The biggest benefit of this approach is that the people in the company start identifying with it. It goes way beyond merely being a place to work; it becomes their company.

The most important person I gave bad news to was my partner. I phoned him on the last day of the month, no matter where in the world he was at the time, and told him how we had done. In the dozen years of our partnership and friendship I don't think I missed that monthly call more than the fingers on one hand.

It wasn't easy; I was in deep trouble; my self-confidence was low and I did not want to have those conversations. In the end it was critical to the survival of our company that I told him because when the chips were really down he helped us through. He never enjoyed the bad news, but without it the trust would not have been there and he would have let us go, and written off his investment.

His was the example I held before me in our staff addresses.

I have to admit that I found it impossible to have this kind of relationship, and to apply these values, in my dealings with DaimlerChrysler. The relationship is so one-sided that it is not a relationship. Dealers are forced to play games, and the shadow life can so easily become reality, and reflect on your dealings with staff and customer, if you do not keep yourself well grounded.

CHAPTER 15.

Dealer Councils.

I have mixed feelings about the effectiveness of dealer councils.

That's a rather unsatisfactory situation considering the experience I have had with them; I initiated the formation of the Mercedes-Benz dealer council whilst I was the board member for marketing; as a dealer I was on the council for over a decade, including a term as chairman, and throughout that time I was chairman of the KwazuluNatal regional council.

Perhaps you will have a better idea by the end of this chapter.

Morris Shenker brooked no opposition from dealers. There was always a moment of anticipation among the dealers at the annual conference when he would be challenged by Brian Schrosbree, the Nelspruit dealer. Maybe Brian relished it as well because very few would pit themselves against the rapier blows of Shenker's replies.

This paranoia was said to come from the early days of his

chairmanship of the company when challenges came thick and fast from the original distributors who resented their loss of independence, and from shareholders Volkskas who would have preferred their own man in the job.

I always sought the opinion of dealers in a number of areas; sales programmes, selection of exterior colours, model selection, volumes; areas where their opinion could be better than ours. In these instances we invited the dealers who had shown the greatest capability in these areas.

These selective groups caused jealousy among some other dealers who felt the dealers selected were singled out for favour. The position was aggravated in that we sometimes felt we would get the best advice from a sales manager, and that put the dealer principal's nose out of joint, even when we asked his approval.

The solution seemed to be to form a dealer council to give the dealers a structured opportunity to have their say. We approached a few senior dealers and with their advice got a group together to think the thing through. They were an outstanding group, successful as dealers, well educated and fully capable of debating any subject at the highest level.

We never had such a group when the council started to be democratically elected and this is one of the failures of dealer councils; the only way to satisfy all is to have an elective process, but when you start to create restrictions on a geographic basis, and restrict the dealer groups to one representative, you do not get the best qualified dealers on the council.

The dealers who led the process in terms of deciding on a constitution and structure were all chartered accountants; Roy McCallister, John Moss, John Mills and Graham Damp.

Graham and Roy served for nearly twenty years; the two John's sold their businesses and moved on.

I remember the early days of that council as a satisfying relationship of almost equals. It is a pity about the "almost" but a dealer can never let his guard down.

We also listened to them; I remember one example when I had to put a major programme on hold; a young researcher had left Toyota and formed his own company to measure customer satisfaction. I was impressed with his system and wanted to introduce it into the network. His name was Albert McClean and we were his first clients.

When the dealers objected, and wanted to consult widely with other dealers it slowed the process down by many months, and forced some changes to the design. I had to make advances to Albert to keep his company going until their revenue stream started.

I remember a magic moment on a trip we took with the entire council to Stuttgart and later to the US (I missed the US leg as I had business that needed me to get back to South Africa). We had a one hour session with the young man who was heading up engineering in Unterturkheim.

We were all struck with his openness, charm and knowledge, and the handle-bar moustache. It was Dieter Zetcher, of course, and I'm sure none of us who were there that day were surprised when he succeeded Jurgen Schrempp as chairman of DaimlerChrysler many years later.

When I became a dealer it was logical to be on the dealer council because I was able to see both points of view, and able to guide both parties around difficulties of understanding. And it certainly worked that way.

Graham Damp was the second chairman of the council and had stayed in that position for way beyond his term because he was seen by the dealers to be courageous and principled, and because he did not believe there was logical successor at that time. The latter reason is evidence of a degree of arrogance, which I was to learn existed when I sold Inyanga Motors to his group years later.

Graham would not let the manufacturer off the hook on matters he believed to be of importance to the dealer body. He persisted with issues when most would have abandoned the cause. In this way he often alienated the manufacturer representatives and, although I admired him for his standing, I knew that his was not always the way to get change.

Throughout the time I worked with Graham I never saw him use his position for the betterment of McCarthy Motors alone; everything was done for the dealer body as a whole; even his strong resistance to DNl, the national parts distribution system I described in the chapter on Christoff Kopke. In fact, Graham's persistence with subjects that the manufacturer was not going to change put his company in jeopardy.

My style when I took over the chairman's role from him was much more conciliatory and inclusive. I had the advantage of knowing what would be unacceptable, and to an extent which buttons to push to get movement.

In pre-meetings I used a debating system learned from de Bono of getting all points of view down on paper before discussing them. And we introduced the system of the "Top Five" dealer concerns, items that would stay on the agenda until resolved, or we agreed to drop them.

The biggest advance we made was to establish a system of functional and regional committees that would feed into the executive dealer council meetings. The functional committees were of the brands; Mercedes-Benz cars, Mercedes-Benz commercial vehicles, Mitsubishi, Chrysler/Jeep/Dodge and Freightliner/Fuso, as well as committees for parts, service, IT and dealer development. These committees comprised the responsible managers from the manufacturer and a selection of dealers who were regarded as those who could contribute the most.

At their best (willing manufacturer representatives, knowledgeable dealers) the committees worked remarkably well. Amongst these were the deliberations of the parts committee while Barry Hastings was the main dealer council representative; we hardly ever had to take issues to the executive; they were resolved at committee level.

Regional meetings were to allow all dealers the opportunity to provide input and were obviously organized along geographic lines to reduce travel time and cost. They covered all aspects of the business and therefore duplicated the work being done in the functional committees.

But it was an important forum to provide feedback to all dealers on what was being achieved in the executive and to share some of the information that the executive members were privy to.

The communication system did not work as well within DaimlerChrysler. Their divisional managers did not attend the executive meetings and we often encountered awkward and frustrating situations where the executive meeting made decisions which were not followed through.

Although the executive meeting was large (nine dealers, about the same number from the manufacturer) I always pleaded for the divisional managers to be present. Had I been one of them I would not have wanted issues affecting my division to be debated, and decisions made, without me being present. One of the arguments against their inclusion was ironical; they didn't have the time.

An issue that infuriated us, and which we could not put a stop to, was the manufacturer's people introducing systems and rules that they claimed the dealer council had approved. Of course we challenged, but I think many of our colleagues truly believed that we had rubber-stamped some of those unpopular changes.

The chairmen who followed me, Mark Philp and Philip Michaux, both did an admirable job in their own styles. Philip had the tough job of being in the chair when new dealer contracts were being introduced, and when the new dealer strategy, which turned the Mercedes-Benz dealer network on its head, was coming into being. I did not envy him those tasks.

Having read this far you will say why the mixed feelings?

It is because no matter what systems you put into place, any democratic process is only as good as the people who operate in it. In my opinion the DaimlerChrysler dealer council became an institution strong on process and weak on decisions.

A footnote is provided by the law makers. We had lawyers sit in on our meetings to ensure we were not behaving in a manner which contravened the competition laws. Their main finding; the word "council" suggests collusion!

Long live the dealer "forums".

Chapter 16.

A value driven organization.

At one of our weekly management meetings I asked the managers what they really wanted out of their jobs, and out of their lives. I encouraged them to think about it and we would discuss it the following week.

It was one of those sessions that really worked, as it often does when you narrow the focus to personal needs. At the end one of them said "And what do you want?"

I hadn't given it much conscious thought, but obviously it had been there for some time because within a moment or two I was able to answer; "I would like our company to have people who are energetic, motivated and disciplined".

That was our first value statement. We had other signs which proclaimed that we wanted to be different, for example our name badges announced "We are proud to be a part of the Inyanga family". But this was our first attempt to say what values were desirable.

From this it was an easy step to a statement of intent for the company;

"We want to be the most attractive and profitable motor dealer in Zululand. We will do so with employees who are energetic, motivated and disciplined, and who have a passion for customers and profit"

In my quarterly addresses to the staff I talked about these values, explaining the words, explaining the benefits of us all behaving this way, not bringing our domestic problems to work, having an inner belief in ourselves, how lack of discipline brought risk.

We re-designed our performance reviews giving equal weighting to job performance and values. We recruited only people who met the profile. We chose a customer champion every few months; they wore a badge with colours reversed from the normal name badge proclaiming "I have been chosen a Customer Champion". It became a very sought after honour.

Despite all there remained a core of people who did not conform to this ideal. I tackled the managers on this issue, saying they were not addressing the few who were spoiling it for the rest of the staff. I asked them to name the staff members who had a bad attitude and they came up with eighteen names.

The next day I met with the eighteen in our training room. I was alone. I told them they had been identified by their managers as having a bad attitude, and I explained what that meant and how it affected the whole company. Then I said, "The way I see it you have three choices. The best choice, and the one I would love you to adopt, is that you recognize this in yourself and you change. If you can't do that you should leave the company and I will accept your resignation after the meeting. The choice I will not accept is that you don't change and you stay with the company; I will not allow you to do that".

Three of that group became outstanding employees, with two of them becoming customer champions. One employee hung around for longer than we should have allowed him, and the rest left within three months of that meeting, unable to stay where they were not welcome.

That move changed the company. Employees were more content and co-operative and our customers received an improved level of service.

I wanted to go even further. At a budget meeting held at the Ithala Game Reserve near Vryheid I came up with a profit sharing concept. The principle was that the owners of the business would be content with a certain level of performance, a measure based on a certain return on sales, and performance above that we would share with the staff. I called it Super Bonus.

Everybody in the company was already on a bonus scheme. If the employee was not in an incentive related job they could receive a bonus equal to 10% of their salary on a monthly basis. This bonus was determined by some performance factor in their department, for example the tea ladies/cleaners in the showrooms received their bonus based on the CSI results for that brand; the admin people received their bonus based on debtor days.

The Super Bonus was to be an over and above bonus, and I had worked out a formula that we could debate. But the Super Bonus could only be earned if the employee behaved according to a set of values; irrespective of performance the employee had to embrace the values deemed to be important to the company.

There was much excitement about this concept and

everyone willingly threw themselves into identifying an expanded set of values. After a long debate we said that was enough, the list was probably too long anyway we should be careful not to complicate the issue. I said Craig Schnell and I would provide an explanation for the values; we would separately do the exercise and have them ready for the following week.

That evening we went on a game drive, all of us in an open game viewing truck. Just down the hill from the main camp we came across two wildebeest and our ranger explained that you could see these were males from the black on their snout, and that they had been expelled from the herd as they were no longer of use.

Eva Jansen, from the back of the truck, in a very loud voice said that was just like our new value system, employees who did not buy into them could depart. Eva did not exactly use those words. She instantly found a name for our values; the Wildebeest Values.

Craig came up with better definitions than mine and we soon had cards printed with a picture of a wildebeest and explanations of the values in English on the one side and Zulu on the other.

Here they are;

Loyal.

Loyal staff would stay in the company through the good and the bad times. They would believe in the values of the company, treat it as their own and be in it for more than just the pay check at the end of the month.

Passionate.

Passionate staff would put their heart into everything they do. Their enthusiasm would be infectious, they would take pride in the work they produce thus making it a high standard.

Energetic.

Energetic staff would be tireless, always on the go, always looking for more work and quick to respond when asked to do something. They will accomplish a lot in a day because everything they take on will be done quickly. You won't ever see them sitting around waiting for time to pass.

Motivated.

Motivated staff believe in themselves and will want to succeed. They will set themselves high standards and want to be the best in their particular job. They will always be looking for better ways to do things.

Unselfish.

Unselfish staff will never say "it's not my job" and will always be prepared to lend a hand. They will be people you can count on to be there when needed. Unselfish people see the big picture.

Team Player.

A team player will work well with others in the department and in the company. They will protect the image of the company and never shove blame onto other people or departments. They will seek to resolve rather than point fingers. They will communicate when there is conflict rather than push things under the rug. They will not speak behind their colleagues back.

Willing to go the extra mile.

A person who will do whatever it takes to get the job done. Going beyond the call of duty for a customer or putting in extra hours at work. A CSI Champion. Here staff would apply the "sunset rule".

Friendly.

Friendly staff will apply the "ten-foot rule" to staff and customers. They will always wear a smile and treat everyone with respect. They will be approachable to both customers and staff and be a pleasure to be around.

Discipline.

Disciplined staff exercise self control in relationships with colleagues and customers. They do not shortcut the company's policies and procedures. They are rarely absent.

Honesty/integrity.

Staff who do not lie to customers or colleagues. They admit their mistakes, accept responsibility and do not cover up. When they say they will do something you can consider it done. What you see is what you get. No hidden agendas.

Sadly the Super Bonus system did not work. There was a payout once and then we went through a period when the company did not even make the minimum level of profit the shareholders needed for growth and reward. It was also too complicated and a nightmare to provide for, to the extent that we never knew what our true profit position was.

The Wildebeest Values are a wonderful set of standards for employee behaviour but too long to be able to remember, and that is a critical element in a value system. In our new company, Tangawizi Motors, we have only three values.

Chapter 17.

A winning formula.

Our management team at Inyanga Motors stayed together for more than 5 years, an unprecedented level of stability.

So how did we create a company that allowed this level of satisfaction among managers? It started with finding or developing competent people to take management positions and that took many years, with many disappointments. Even at the end not all of the managers were of equal calibre, one or two were even average, but there was a core of exceptional people and they pulled the others along.

Once we had a group of managers with the competence to run the company we all developed together. We were constantly questioning and improving systems, changing incentive structures, improving our own management skills. These developments took place in a structure.

It started with the weekly meeting, in exactly the same way I used this forum with my management team at DaimlerChrysler, forcing integration and resolution of relationship problems, discussing the business, communicating on a wide variety of issues within the business, the community and our industry.

But the most important structure was the four-monthly budget meetings. I do not believe a small retail motor business has the acumen to forecast beyond a short time frame so we always did an annual budget and amended it every four months. That was the first purpose of the budget meeting, to review and change the numbers and learn business principles from the process, but we almost always used this forum to improve our company and ourselves in broader areas.

Sometimes the extra thing I introduced was deceptively simple, like the time I asked everyone to write down what they liked best about each of their colleagues. That forced them to take a lateral view of some of the people they had no time for. In the end that exercise was an excellent team building intervention.

The art of defending your budget was also always a challenging matter for each of the managers. I did not fully succumb to using electronic media to assist with the budget approval process because by forcing each manager to defend his case, and making them look incompetent if their argument was not logical, they improved their knowledge and emotional control.

I always found it amusing that some of them wanted me to "just take a look" at their calculations before the meeting, hoping to avoid the public scrutiny. Some of our managers had no formal management or financial training; the budget process gave them all a broader understanding of the business.

As I explained in an earlier chapter, I am an avid reader of business books and many of the business philosophies I read about became the subject of debate at a budget meeting.

We went through the Jack Welch period, and the Wal-Mart lessons (our ten-foot and sunset rules came from there) and the way Ackermann made his stores different.

I did not only manage through the group, I also dealt with non-performance on a one-on-one basis and luckily two of the three managers who received letters of warning calling for specific improvement were able to change their game. The third one was leaving the company and I let it ride.

The managers also had their bonus structure changed every four months. Sometimes the changes were quite large. I knew this was unfair because of the uncertainty it brought about, but I believe the bonus structure is the best way to induce the right behaviour and there always seemed to be new priorities for the business. No doubt this practise also made them more flexible.

It will be quite clear that my leadership style evolved over time but did not stray far from a number of general principles;

. **Give as much freedom as possible.** The manager needs to feel that their department is their own invention. One of the ways of doing this was to pay bonuses on nett profit so that they can manipulate the cost and revenue dimensions. This can only happen at a mature stage in their understanding of the finances in their section (in our current company, with young managers unschooled in these matters, we are still at the stage of paying a portion of the bonus for cost control).

. **Control the risk areas strongly.** Balancing the freedom you wish to give your managers must be a risk control structure. This might sound like a contradiction in philosophy but I believe very strongly in a minimum of controls, at the key areas of risk (vehicle sales, debtors, warranty, cash), and that these controls are never compromised. For many of the rules it becomes a dismissible offence to break them. The funny thing is, when you know the rules and obey them, it leaves you free to employ your energy elsewhere.

. Provide forums for frequent communication. Management is a team game and is built on trust and understanding. There can and should be a place for variations in individual style, but not at the expense of the common good; the weekly meetings and quarterly budget meetings provide the forums to iron out these differences.

. Live the values. The values of a business need to be appropriate to the circumstances including customer expectations, employee ideals and society ethics. Then you need to live them from the top. They provide the foundation for many decisions. When you ask yourself "what is the right thing to do?" the answer should be enlightened by your value system. At Inyanga, when we had a simple set of values; energy, motivation and discipline, we looked for those values in all staff we interviewed for positions in the company.

. Ensure accountability. Nothing kills a team faster than individuals who will not be held accountable for their actions or the actions of their subordinates. When I joined UCDD I was struck by the lack of defined accountability. When things went wrong no-one was responsible and as a result it was almost impossible to get things done across departmental lines. The tools of job descriptions and performance appraisals help greatly in this regard, but only if they are consistently applied and visibly supported by management.

. Keep changing. Complacency is not an option in the modern motor industry; it will inevitably lead to reduced standards and performance and to business failure. Of course, in business as in life, complacency does not get a look-in when the chips are down. When times are tough most employees up their game and I promote this by giving honest assessments of the financial status of the company at my quarterly company address. When times are prosperous the drive is on for higher performance on an individual and departmental basis; in this regard the availability of best practise data is invaluable in keeping people striving to do better. The management bonus structure is the most important tool in changing strategy and performance.

Chapter 18.

Dealer of the Year programmes.

We won our first Dealer of the Year award because Standard Bank decided they owned the customer.

It has become a standing joke, this who owns the customer game. The banks think they own the customers. So do the insurance companies, medical aid societies, airlines, and the big stores. And of course the manufacturers and their dealers come close to blows over the issue.

Today, even Government thinks they own the customers and must protect grown people from making decisions on credit.

Standard Bank, who were the third player in motor financing, but considerably smaller then the big two Wesbank and ABSA (then marketed as Bankfin, a name they foolishly dropped), decided to by-pass the motor dealers and market their finance and insurance products directly to their customer base.

The strategy flopped, but not before it brought to us one of the best F&I people in the country. Eva Jansen was the office manager for Standard's motor financing division in Empangeni, one of the branches they closed down.

When she came to Inyanga Motors she brought her sidekick Rita Reddy. And she brought integrity and passion to our finance and insurance business. She also became a key person in our control of risk in vehicle sales, a role I valued and supported by giving her equal management status and final sign-off on all deals.

So it should have come as no surprise at the DOTY awards ceremony at Sun City in 2004, that Inyanga Motors name appeared as one of the five nominees for best DaimlerChrysler Services dealer of 2003. The joy of winning it that year, and receiving the congratulations of our peers, was one of the treasures in my life as a motor dealer. It gave us a taste for more.

Unfortunately the DaimlerChrysler Services competition did not meet the criteria that I believe are essential for a DOTY competition; simplicity, transparency and aligned to the manufacturer's strategy as expressed in their reward programme.

Years later I said to Kerry Elsdon, a Canadian who was running DaimlerChrysler Services at that time, and a big corporate games-player; "We never knew why we won your DOTY programme and the next time we win it we also won't know why." He promised clarity but never delivered on that promise.

A dealer of the year programme can be a tremendous motivator for dealers. But if it measures the wrong things it will receive no standing. You can tell the difference; when the guy walking to the podium is seen to be a really good dealer by his peers the congratulations are warm and enthusiastic. I've seen the opposite, and it is embarrassing.

For many years, in the Dealer Council, we tried to persuade DaimlerChrysler to change the rules of their programme to fit their strategy. The trouble with the manufacturer is every department wants to have their issues included and it becomes an unfocused programme not given the time of day by dealers.

Manufacturers really only want three things; they want you to sell their products by the bucket-load, they want you to satisfy customers and they want you to do what they tell you to do (euphemistically called "standards").

When DCSA started rewarding these three things, in terms of kick-backs when you excelled in them, it became an easy step to persuade them to also measure these things in their DOTY programme. This way we made points towards DOTY at the same time as we made money. The reward became aligned to the strategy.

The DaimlerChrysler Services award for 2003 was a departmental award, it wasn't one of the big ones, the category awards, or the biggest of all, the "Chairman's Award" which is for the single dealer judged to be the best that year.

We started motivating our team towards one of these prized awards. The Services award made us realise that it was possible and, in that way, it played a tremendous part in our later successes. We talked about it endlessly in management meetings, we waited with keen anticipation for the monthly score sheets and we published the figures on company notice boards.

We got our first big one in the beautiful setting of The Castle on the Cape Town foreshore. Results for all dealers had been published until October so we knew our standing at that time. For the last two months of the year we only knew our own numbers. It was a sure thing that we had the Chrysler/

Jeep prize, but the Mercedes passenger and Mitsubishi prizes were a very close thing and we were out of the running for the Mercedes commercial vehicle award.

The ceremonies are not fun. There's too much anxiety. You know that your managers back home haven't gone to bed, waiting for that SMS. You think you know the result but there is that nagging doubt, and you don't want to jinx it. Your friends are telling you this is your time. Not fun.

We were adjudged the best Chrysler/Jeep dealer in South Africa for 2004. We didn't make the other two so the Chairman's award went to an outstanding dealer, Rola Motors, whose business is just 35 kilometres from the place where we celebrated their triumph.

When my wife and I returned to our business the next day all of the staff (and some of the suppliers and the banks) were in the foyer to greet and cheer us. Quite an emotional time and testimony to the successful communications we had run in the company and the community.

The next one was in Cairo.

We arrived in the early hours of the morning to be greeted by the noxious smell of car fumes. In that city the air is so still, and the traffic so dense, that the pollution is truly life threatening, even at two in the morning.

The ceremony was to have been held in a monster tent erected for the occasion alongside the pyramids. A few hours before the event a desert storm came up, accompanied by tremendous winds which lifted the tent and smashed it back onto the prepared feast, causing thousands of rands of damage. Fortunately no-one was injured; a few hours later and it would have been a different story.

The venue was switched to the hotel we were staying in, the Sheraton, on an island in the Nile River. They did an exemplary job at short notice but a lot of the flavour was lost without the audio visuals.

The 2005 programme had introduced new categories, Dealers were grouped according to size and only the five big city dealers, called brand centres were also judged by vehicle brands. We were in the middle category called market centres.

We knew we would win our category, and we did, but it was the "Chairman's Award" that we aspired to. Dr Hansgeorg Niefer, Chairman of DaimlerChrysler South Africa did the announcement;

"Although all the dealers who won their categories did an excellent job, in the end there were two outstanding dealers, Inyanga Motors and the Mercedes-Benz brand centre, Durban. We decided on the one which has done the most to advance our new dealer strategy. The award goes to the Mercedes-Benz brand centre, Durban".

There you have it. For "advance our new dealer strategy" he meant they had spent R129 million on their new building. The disappointment was considerably reduced because I am a great admirer of Yunus Akoo, the joint owner of the brand centre and his manager at the time, Brian Harvey, who today is running Inyanga Motors.

We finally won it the next year in the Aquarium in Durban's uShakaLand. It was an unsuitable place as we were seated along two branches of the venue so that we could not see all of the attendees. And it was way too crowded.

The winner of the "Chairman's Award" is invited to say a few words, and this is what I said;

"This is a wonderful moment for us, and there will be great celebration in Empangeni tonight. I know Hugh O'Mahoney, sitting over there, will also be pleased. He can stop saying: I wish you would win the damn thing Cleary so that you can start making money!

Well, even Hugh knows that the DCSA programme does allow you to make money, and I congratulate and thank DCSA for changing the programme to something we can admire and strive for.

I have to acknowledge some people who should also share in this award, because without them we wouldn't have survived.

It is not common knowledge, but we lost money for many, many years and during that time we were under tremendous pressure. We were on DCSA's problem dealer list for many years and I know there were concerns about our floor plan and even proposals to cancel us. One senior manager at DCSA would not let them do it.

The banks wanted to cancel our overdraft. Fortunately for me, one of my best friends was at that time a director and senior manager at the bank and he gave us reprieve.

At that time cash flow was everything, ahead of profit. So getting extended credit terms on parts was more important than buying smart. One dealer, who knew of our difficulties, believed in us enough to give us 60-day and then 90-day terms. The dealer was McCarthy, Pinetown and the people who helped us were Graham Damp and Brian Harvey.

But all of this did not help us and the time came when I had to phone my financial partner and tell him we had to close, we couldn't even pay the salaries. He told me to do nothing, came down to Empangeni, sat in my office and wrote me a cheque for R2 million rand. He told me we could repay it when we could afford to, without interest.

And finally, even more than our earthly friends, we are grateful for the help we received from God".

Chapter 19.

The Competitions Commission.

I was saddened when Toyota paid an administrative fine of R10 million for vertical collusion with their dealers. Saddened that they did not fight the principle of whether vertical collusion should be a misdemeanour in a franchise system, and saddened because it confirmed the perception of the general public that the motor industry is a rip off.

The Competition Commission announced that they were investigating the motor industry for price fixing, that is, horizontal collusion between the motor manufacturers and importers and at the same time investigating incidents of vertical price fixing between manufacturers and their dealers.

It is the latter that I believe should not be controlled by competition law when it occurs in a franchise situation.

The commission's investigation was triggered by a number of reports appearing in the press throughout the country that cars were more expensive in South Africa than in certain other countries. One such report led to the Toyota investigation; it appeared in a Cape Town newspaper and was a letter to the paper from a reader who said the Toyota Corolla was cheaper in Australia.

The investigation uncovered the fact that Toyota had told their dealers that they could not discount the new Corolla.

You have to ask yourself, why did a manufacturer tell their dealers not to discount a car? Surely fewer cars would be sold if there was no discount, and how could the manufacturer do something that would result in the sale of less cars?

There were two reasons. Firstly it transpired that Toyota decided to reduce the mark-up to their dealers for the new Corolla from 16% to 10%. They wanted the new car to come in at an excellent price relative to the outgoing model and, after investing hundreds of millions to make the new car in their Durban plants they could not attain this price target without reducing the dealer margin.

If the dealer was then to discount the car even further, and erode the profit margin of 10%, it would reduce overall dealer profit in a dangerous way. Dangerous because unprofitable dealers cannot give the level of service Toyota is renowned for, and dangerous because dealer margins are slim to start with; today best practise among South African new franchise motor dealers (best practise meaning the results obtained from the top 10% of dealers) is a 2,8% return on sales; that means that the best dealers in the country make R2,80 for every R100 of sales.

So their first reason to issue instructions which would result in them selling fewer cars was to preserve dealer profitability.

The second reason was not to damage the image of the car. There is nothing that cheapens the image of a car, and reduces its resale value more than excessive discounting. And tell me why a motor manufacturer, with an infrastructure the size of a small country cannot protect the image of its product to ensure its future?

I am today involved with Renault, a fine product with the best safety record in the European NCAP, and innovative designs. A few years ago Renault embarked on an aggressive campaign of discounting to increase their market share. One scheme followed another until eventually you could not sell the car without some form of assistance. The result was a drop in the resale value of the cars to a degree far in excess of the discount that was being received on the car.

Fewer sales and lower dealer profits have had an effect on Renault that will last for many years. They have lost dealers, meaning many have lost jobs and there is less service for customers. Renault is an excellent company and they will recover but they surely wish they had continued with a steady conquest of the South African market rather than the unseemly haste which set their product back many years.

So who benefited from Renault's market assault? The customer who today cannot realise his expected value on trade-in? The dealer? The manufacturer?

So why can't a manufacturer control the price of his product and in so doing control its image and the financial health of its dealers?

To come back to the Toyota example, nobody has adequately dealt with the issue of cars being cheaper elsewhere. I have seen some reports of studies done but no-one least of all the consumer wants to know the uncomfortable truth; between one quarter and one-third of a cars price structure in South Africa is made up by government's tax and duty structure. When I say least of all the consumer it is because even though we love to bash the government, we love to bash motor dealers even more.

And in reducing the mark-up from 16% to 10% Toyota were merely following other motor manufacturers and importers. Most cars have a mark-up today of an average of 8%, from lows of 5% on entry level models to around 12%.

The Competition Commission then turned their attention to DaimlerChrysler and their super fleet rebate; a practise of giving kickbacks to dealers for the sale of cars to major fleets and government.

The scheme worked like this; if a dealer was selling to a super fleet they could claim an extra kickback to help them with the sale. The amount of the kickback was equal to 2% of the wholesale value of the car. Initially instructions said this was dependant on the dealer giving no more than a 3% discount in total to the customer, later, when cars became more readily available, the limitation was dropped.

As a part of their investigation the Competitions Commission approached Inyanga Motors and asked for records of all transactions of sales to super fleets, and, as I was a member of the dealer council I was required to give copies of all records of council meetings as well as meetings of dealers in the KwazuluNatal region.

Our records of sales transactions showed no pattern whatsoever; discounts varied with almost every deal.

And this raises another issue regarding discounts. You can give a customer a great deal with no discount by improving the offer on his trade-in. It is often forgotten that when there is a trade-in involved the customer should always look at the final figures; the difference he must pay between the offer on his trade-in and the price of the new vehicle. We would sometimes have customers responding to only one element (normally being offered a discount up front over the phone) and paying more than the deal we had offered.

So in our deals to super fleet customers there was also the element of a trade-in which affected the discount we gave.

DaimlerChrysler paid an administrative fine on behalf of themselves and their dealers and the sadness I had felt when Toyota did not fight the principle of vertical price fixing in a franchise system was heightened tenfold.

Can Pick n Pay decide what price to charge on an item in all their stores? What about gym fees in Virgin Active or the price of a particular book at Exclusive Books?

Why can't a manufacturer or importer tell their dealers at what price they can sell their cars, specially when in doing so they protect the customer's value of the product they are purchasing and guarantee future service?

There are more than 500 car models on sale in South Africa today. It is the most competitive industry in the country. A customer is spoiled for choice; if he is not happy with your price structure he can always buy another brand.

I was so aggrieved by the damage the Competitions Commission was doing to the image of the motor industry that I decided to run a cost price campaign at Inyanga Motors. The inspiration came from one of Ackermann's books, in which he describes their pricing on specials, calling them "islands of loss in a sea of profit".

It was obviously not going to be a sustainable programme; we are in business to make a profit and if other dealers responded it would hurt the image of the cars and future resale value. We offered to sell at cost (and offered to prove the claim by showing the manufacturer's invoice) Mercedes-

Benz A-Class in month one, Jeep Cherokee in month two and our entire Mitsubishi range in month three.

We sold cars on the programme, but that wasn't the point, we wanted to show customers how very small our margin is, and they were amazed. One customer said to my wife "Can't you do better than that?"

Chapter 20.

The good and bad of the franchise system.

We were in a dealer council meeting with the manufacturer, and the argument was about who was to pay for an expensive data line between dealer and manufacturer. Dr. Hansgeorg Niefer, their Chairman, had argued that analysis showed that traffic on the line was almost all dealer traffic.

I argued back; "Dr. Niefer we don't want to use that line. We use it to order cars directly from Germany which used to be your function, now we do it. We also use that line to process applications for customer credit; that is another function that we took over from you and in doing so it allowed you to reduce your headcount while we increased ours".

"Well then", he said, "you should pay a percentage of the hundreds of millions we spend on developing new systems."

"Please understand', I persisted, "your system priorities are almost entirely different to ours. We mainly need systems for accounts and parts. Integration into your systems is more to your advantage than to ours. Already we are compromising our needs to support what you want."

The argument went on for much longer and we ended up paying for the data line. The story illustrates the gap between wholesale and retail and the dominant position of the manufacturer. And it is that dominance that causes the worst ills of the franchise system in the motor industry. At best it is a system of patronage, at worst it is a military dictatorship.

Another example. I was driving through an older part of Empangeni and recognised a building that used to be a part of the Ritchie organisation, and I remembered first meeting Allister Ritchie in that building in the early 80's.

Then my thoughts jumped to the new facility they had completed in Empangeni and the facility they were planning for Richards Bay and it occurred to me that such capital expenditure could overextend them and they could lose their business. And I argued with myself, why doesn't the manufacturer value the wonderful image Ritchie has built up over 30 years, why would they jeopardise such a good and loyal business by forcing them to invest in new facilities?

In a system of patronage they would delay the expenditure, in a military dictatorship they would not be allowed to decide on the best timing. I hope for Ritchie's sake the former prevails.

Inyanga Motors is still one of the best looking buildings in Zululand, and it is certainly the best facility for a motor dealership. Yet we were required to comply with the latest corporate identity design being implemented worldwide. It did not matter that the design would bring little added value to the business. It did not matter that the design was not suitable for a hot climate country because of the massive glass walls. It did not matter that we were their best dealer for three years running and didn't need a new building to prove our worth. We had to change; and for a cost estimated at R30 million with no contribution from the manufacturer.

So they lost me as a dealer; I sold the business.

But there is hope for DaimlerChrysler dealers. The manufacturer decided to enter into retail themselves and purchased the dealers in Cape Town and parts of Johannesburg. And they put their money where their mouth was and invested heavily in new facilities. Right now they are probably losing a bundle and getting to know the pitfalls of retail a little better.

The question of whether a manufacturer or importer should have their own dealerships is always the subject of debate when dealers come together. The fear is that the manufacturer will favour their own dealerships, and they undoubtedly do. The counter argument is that they understand retail better and will probably give dealers a fairer shake. I certainly favour the latter argument as it is what I find in being an independent dealer with franchises controlled by AMH.

The manufacturer does not only bring unnecessary cost to the dealer, they bring massive increases in complexity. Not least of the many manufacturer initiatives which add complexity to the dealer is the manufacturer's standards programme.

When I was a DaimlerChrysler dealer the standards were audited bi-annually, they now are being inspected every six weeks. Can you imagine the resources required to administer more than 100 standards and keep them up to scratch for a six-weekly inspection cycle?

In the dealer council we advocated to the manufacturer standards that measured outputs, not standards that told the dealers how to do their jobs; specially when those doing the telling had a poor understanding of the retail business. I come back to the chapter on DOTY programmes; the manufacturer should be measuring the dealers' market share and customer satisfaction. If he is selling the cars and satisfying the customers what more do you want?

Plenty, unfortunately.

So why do I carry on being a dealer, what is the good in the franchise system? It's simple; I love the motor retail business and the constant variety of handling such a diverse range of activities. I love selling cars. And sometimes you can make decent money doing these things.

If I have to deal with manufacturers and importers to get to what I love doing, then so be it.

A final word to the biggest franchise holder in the country, the government; please understand that Franchise South Africa is growing a level of cost and complexity to rival the motor manufacturers. I could handle the one, I'm not sure I want to be in business if I have to handle both.

CHAPTER 21.

Selling Inyanga Motors.

I had hoped to work in the company until I was 70 years of age, and was making plans to ensure I could do so by giving myself a lesser role. I planned to move my office upstairs when we did the alterations to the building. There was to be a suite of offices, one of which was to be mine, one Cathy's if she wished to continue in the business, and the third Cheryl's. Cheryl would be one of three people reporting to me, and she would continue to be the accountant and to be responsible for staff functions such as personnel and IT.

The other two people reporting to me were to be the two DP's in Empangeni and Vryheid, the two operational heads. I planned to give Craig Schnell the Empangeni job. First he needed to tackle this job at a lesser level, and I asked him to take the job of running Vryheid.

It seemed like a nice orderly plan, and was supported by the commonly held belief that the 2010 Soccer World Cup would give a tremendous boost to the South African economy. But a voice of doubt was flitting around asking for entrance; Cathy was openly questioning me and looking for assurances that we could manage the tremendous capital investments required to change our facilities.

Then the possibility of selling was given a promotion from a most unexpected quarter. I attended a meeting in the Cradle of Mankind which DaimlerChrysler called to provide an introduction to black dealer shareholders of their role in the network. I attended with Sheila Ngubane who had become a 25% shareholder of ours with the assistance of funds from the trust which DaimlerChrysler and the dealers had established for this purpose, and with a loan provided by ABSA.

After dinner Fritz von Olst, Theo Swanepoel and I had one of those sessions where you talk interminably late into the evening. The primary subject was the change to our industry brought about by government and what we had observed in the black shareholder meeting of that day. Then, as if by pre-arrangement, they both began telling me I should think very seriously about selling Inyanga Motors; the company was at a peak, we had just won the Chairman's prize as the best dealer in the country, we were making reasonable profits.

Cathy and I discussed it; if we did not sell at that time we would have to incur the capital expenditure required to refurbish the buildings in Empangeni and we would have to purchase land (something which was proving to be almost impossible because of municipal apathy in land development) and build in Vryheid. Only after the changes to the company's facilities were completed would another opportunity to sell present itself and that would not be before 2009.

In the meantime we would not enjoy decent financial results because of the disruption to our operations during the building phase. The following year, 2007 could be another good year, but it would be followed by a few difficult years. I discussed it in confidence with our other shareholders with a mixed reaction; Sheila and her husband, who was out visiting from Japan where he is currently serving as Ambassador, were in favour, my silent partner was not.

We decided to sell and I approached potential buyers; four in total. One of them was a lead given to me by DaimlerChrysler after I had advised them of our intentions. The lead from DaimlerChrysler must have thought he was buying a chicken run and his overtures were quickly discarded. One was an old friend, but he was not tempted as he was considering extricating himself as well. The other two were groups, the kind of people who wanted to buy more DaimlerChrysler dealerships but whose bid might well be turned down by DaimlerChrysler because they did not want the groups to have more power than they already had.

I approached Philip Michaux at Imperial and Graham Damp at McCarthy's. Both were very interested, Philip thought their best opportunity of success with DaimlerChrysler was to buy the company through an affiliated black-owned company. He gave me the name of the person who would be contacting me soon from that company; he never did.

Graham and I began the months of discussion and negotiation that these processes invariably take.

One of the difficult points of selling was my role with McCarthy's after the sale. Graham wanted continuity and wanted me to stay on for some years. It wasn't ideal but I was resolved to do so if it became a condition of sale. Then another unexpected twist occurred.

The trip winners of the Dealer of the Year competition were treated to a marvellous holiday with our wives and two hosts from DaimlerChrysler; it included several days on a small yacht in the Mediterranean off the coast of Turkey. Brian Harvey was one of the winners and he found an opportunity to tell Cathy that he did not see a future for himself in his present position; he wished he could find an opportunity where he could become a shareholder.

It was just what we wanted. Brian is an outstanding operator, he had worked for Graham Damp when he was running McCarthy Pinetown and I knew Graham had an excellent relationship with him, and he was definitely the kind of man I would feel comfortable leaving in charge of our company. Graham had to negotiate with Bidvest to allow Brian to purchase 10% of the company but was successful in his efforts.

The next hurdle was DaimlerChrysler. I phoned Sascha Gaeda and said I wished to see him and Fritz to discuss the sale. It happened that they were flying to Namibia the next day and could arrange to meet me at Johannesburg airport.

They were pretty devastated to hear that the buyer was McCarthy's because they were not sure it would be approved by the dealer executive committee which was chaired by Dr. Niefer. The committee had previously resolved not to allow certain of the groups with high levels of representation to grow; McCarthy's was one of them. I had my arguments ready, the most telling of which was that independent dealers could no longer afford their franchise with its ridiculous facility standards. In the end I said; "Look Fritz, I sincerely hope that all I have done for our mutual business for over 20 years will not be overlooked for some obscure strategic advantage".

Obscure or not Niefer did not have a problem with the sale.

We had to tell our managers and staff. It was going to be

the hardest hurdle of them all. We stage managed it as carefully as we could; I arranged to have a budget meeting to coincide with the Bidvest board meeting where the final decision was to be made. Our budget meeting was at a game lodge north of Hluhluwe and all afternoon I was on tenterhooks waiting for the call from Graham to confirm the sale.

Eventually I heard after 5 p.m. The managers were all in the meeting room wondering why I kept delaying the progress of the meeting. We ordered drinks and when all were settled I told them the news. It was extremely emotional. Only Cheryl and Craig knew, for the rest it was a complete surprise; in the end I had been able to keep something from them.

The next day we had a series of briefing meetings in Empangeni and Vryheid to allow me to tell all the staff personally, explain my reasons, provide reassurance over the choice of McCarthy's and give the advantages to working for a large company. Within a week we had McCarthy people giving them presentations about the company and the benefits they would enjoy as McCarthy employees. Brand Pretorius drove up from Durban to meet the managers and provide further reassurance in his sincere convincing way.

Already, of course, it was no longer our company. No longer the living entity we had created.

Final.

Tangawizi.

Andrew was waiting for us when Cathy and I and our two daughters Susan and Caryn emerged from the arrivals terminal into the bustle of the crowded streets and the oppressive heat of Zanzibar. He had flown from London the previous day through Dar es Salaam and had that morning taken the ferry across from the mainland. He had a taxi waiting for us, it made South African taxis look positively modern, and we were to learn that it leaked both dust and rain water when it took us north a few days later.

We checked into our hotel in Stone Town and went exploring; down to the seaside and onwards to the square where the night restaurants would emerge in a few hours time. The heat drove us into a cafe with high ceilings and cooling fans. We ordered ginger beer, our favourite drink, and the waiter looked blank. One of us thought to say "Stoney" which struck a chord of memory; "Ah tangawizi" he said.

And so we found the name for our second business in another obscure and romantic location. Tangawizi is the Swahili name for the root ginger and we needed it to add spice to the name for our new businesses.

During the years Inyanga Motors was a marginal business I could not maintain my shareholding. Eventually my partner and I did a deal in which he obtained the majority shares in our company which held the Daihatsu, Renault and Hyundai franchises. As he did not live in Zululand, and was often out of the country I acted as chairman of this company, and for this duty I was credited with 10% of the shares. We always had the unspoken belief that I would buy back a majority of this business when Inyanga Motors was sold. It was more than an option, it was an obligation, and I exercised it.

But the company had an awful name; DAU Motor Holdings (the DAU being the first two and last letter in Daihatsu). The individual franchises traded under the names Zululand Daihatsu, Zululand Renault and Zululand Hyundai, but there was no popular name to provide a unifying brand for the employees and customers. In addition I bought the Honda dealership from colleagues and their staff needed to be brought into the fold.

When we returned from our Zanzibar holiday I asked our auditors to register two companies, one called Tangawizi Motors for our franchised motor businesses and the other Tangawizi Retail Holdings in the event we decided to pursue any other opportunities in products or property that might become available.

Our auditors also put me in touch with Adams and Adams to do trademark registrations and I dealt with a very efficient woman named Samantha Copeling. We wanted the name registered in motor sales and servicing, in jewellery, clothing and alcoholic beverages (because of the excellent shandy made from a combination of beer and ginger beer). All of the names were registered with the exception of the beverage because of a similarity to other beverage products;

to our surprise Tangawizi was not registered by the Coca Cola Company for the drink of this name which they sell in East Africa.

Our Tangawizi brew, as we called the shandy, became the drink of choice at John and Val (Cathy's middle sister) Thorp's game farm in the Ellisras district where we spent a celebratory few days over the New Year which brought in 2007. Celebratory but also with a tinge of sadness; it was the end of an era for both families; they had sold the model farm they had built up for more than a decade. Another outstanding farmer was leaving the land because of the threat of land claims.

The Thorp's, and another couple who were at the farm, were caught up in our enthusiasm for our new venture, and specially the intriguing name. By then Cathy and I had already decided that the gingerbread man, and the line from the nursery rhyme "run, run as fast as you can" would be the symbol and pay-off line for our new company. I had done numerous Google searches and had already done some sketches of a running ginger bread man.

We were beginning to think Tangawizi was born out of parties with friends and family. We went skiing with friends in Lech, Austria and I was still weaving my magic tales of our new name. It was just a few weeks later but already we had cemented in our minds the way we would promote the new name both within the company and to the Zululand public. The pay-off line 'run, run." had such positive connotations of energy; the energy our staff could exercise on behalf of our customers. Our friends were probably bemused at this outpouring of creativity taking place at what should have been my slowdown phase!

We were fortunate to find a young graphic arts student,

Minette Janse van Rensburg who has a way with animated cartoons. She understood my brief completely and soon we had a wonderfully energetic and happy gingerbread man. Minette did not know what to charge for her designs; I asked her to speak to her teacher and get his advice. I paid her double what she asked and also obtained a release on the ownership of the work from her.

Soon there were ads announcing a new grouping of motor brands in Zululand. A second round of ads provocatively asked "Would you like to help us build a great company?"

Tangawizi has been launched into a very rocky economic climate. Since the middle of 2007 vehicle sales have registered levels up to 25% below the previous year. In an industry with low margins the sales reductions can be devastating and we will have to tread very carefully for the next months to negotiate a safe channel.

In the midst of the gloom of the day came an amazing achievement; our Renault dealership was awarded the Renault Global Quality Award for 2007; the best dealer in the country for customer satisfaction and standards. It will do much for self-belief in the coming months.

Two weeks later in an award ceremony held in Swaziland our Hyundai dealership was judged to be the second best independent Hyundai dealer in the country.

So here we go again, running as fast as we can.

Mtunzini.
December, 2008.